Graduate and Grow Rich

The Ultimate Guide
To A
Successful Journey

Dave Bedard

First Edition

Portions of the proceeds from each book go to the Bedard Charitable Fund for scholarships and faculty development.

Success Journey Publishing
Oxford, Massachusetts

Graduate and Grow Rich
The Ultimate Guide to a Successful Journey
By Dave Bedard

Published by:
Success Journey Publishing
Post Office Box 27
Oxford, MA 01540
Order Toll Free 1-866-258-4873
www.graduateandgrowrich.com

Unattributed quotes are by Dave Bedard

Copyright 2008 by David Bedard
Printed in the United States of America

Library of Congress Cataloging-Publication Data

Library of Congress Control Number: 2008900056

Bedard, Dave.
Graduate and Grow Rich:
The Ultimate Guide to a Successful Journey/ Dave Bedard-1st ed.
Includes bibliographical references

1.Career advice
2.Life skills
3.Real world lessons
4.Interview techniques
5.Online jobsites

ISBN 978-0-9814792-2-4

Dedication

*To my wonderful wife Linda
Your support, encouragement and love are
the ingredients that make my journey "rich."
I would not be who I am without your priceless
companionship. You are the love of my life.*

*To Noelle
You are beautiful inside and out. I am blessed
to have you as my daughter. I look forward
to watching you live your dreams.*

*To Josh
You are a special son. I am excited watching
you grow into the man you were born to be.
You are becoming a difference maker through
your passion to help others.*

TABLE OF CONTENTS

Acknowledgments

When asked by a student at the JA Academy "How long it took to write this book," my reply was "It took about one year to write, and a lifetime to compose." Therefore, there are so many who make up the pieces of this composition.

First, I wish to thank the many mentors who have shared their wisdom with me. Some of them probably never knew the impact their willingness to share would have.

To Bob Fouracre, my first mentor, Big Brother, and most of all, life-long friend--You *are* "Superlative."

To John DiPietro for planting the seed in me to write this book. Your guidance and encouragement during the process have made the journey a "success."

To my friends at Worcester State College, especially Dr. Janelle Ashley, Tom McNamara, and Dr. Pat Donovan. Thank you for taking some of your precious time to review this book and offer invaluable input.

To Deb Hopkins, President of Junior Achievement of Central Massachusetts: Your excellent communication skills and willingness to share them have made this book a more valuable tool for our future leaders.

To Josh Tooley for an outstanding cover design.

To each of my first rate reviewers: Tom Cowell, Susan Cowell, Richard Law, Rod Lee, Peter McClintock, Dalia McClintock, John Phillips and Patti Phillips.

Thank you all from the bottom of my heart.

ABOUT THE AUTHOR

Throughout his career, Dave Bedard has mentored hundreds of students and professionals. Inside *Graduate and Grow Rich*, he shares twelve essential life skills that are prevailing attributes of high-achievers, such as being an overcomer, developing a healthy self-esteem and maintaining a positive attitude.

Dave's journey had a humble beginning. Having grown up in a low-income public housing project, he persisted to become a first generation college graduate. With his business degree in hand, he launched a fast-track career as a television advertising executive, becoming a top producer at a major network affiliate.

The "journey" accelerated as Dave opened his own marketing and advertising companies. The combination of entrepreneurial spirit, along with a resolve to *never* go back to "The Project" drove him to grow his ventures to financial independence.

Dave spent two decades conducting leadership training across America and in over twenty-five countries. He is an active contributor on college campuses, serving on numerous boards, as a director, advisor and guest lecturer. He is also a proud member of the Junior Achievement Board in Massachusetts.

"My work on campus made me realize that today's students fear what is next. If we build a bridge of belief...a glimpse of what the world is looking for from them, then, perhaps, they will believe in themselves enough to go out with a healthy self-esteem and make the world a better place."

"There is so much time and money invested in education. We NEED to help them put their best foot forward and continue to put one in front of the other until they are living their dreams. This is still the Land of Opportunity." Dave adds: *"Being an entrepreneur has allowed me to see the world. If a kid from the project can do it, anyone can."*

He and his wife, Linda, have four children and three grand-children. They reside in Massachusetts and Florida.

INTRODUCTION

Have Fun—Grow Rich—Make a Difference...

That's my motto. While the journey is important, enjoying it is *just* as important. I hope that you will *"GROW RICH"* in *every way,* which is why I have written this book.

As you make plans to transition from the classroom to the rest of your life, you have put yourself in a strong position to succeed. According to the Department of Education, the typical bachelor's degree recipient earns about sixty-one percent more over a forty-year working life than those who just graduate from high school. Further, the expected lifetime earnings "premium" of college graduates who earn a higher degree is *over one million dollars more* than high school graduates.

The rules in the "work world," however, are different. The corridors of corporate America demand a different skill set than the hallowed halls of academia.

Back in the day, employers would look at new grads as apprentices, taking them under their wing, grooming them and teaching the skills required to prosper in "their world": what to wear, inter-office communication, proper attitude/etiquette, etc.

Those coddling, bottle-feeding days are gone. We are in the middle of a transitional economy, one in which so many of the jobs that were once havens for grads, now have been outsourced to foreign countries, and the competition for remaining jobs is fierce.

Our twenty-first century reality is that many companies now view new college grads as hiring risks. Employers don't have the time, money or patience to teach the practical life skills needed to bridge the gap between the two worlds. They prefer to screen and hire those who already have developed these valued skills.

"The purpose of life, after all, is to live it, to taste-experience to the utmost, to reach out eagerly and without fear for newer and richer experiences." **Eleanor Roosevelt**

ARE YOU READY?

"A single conversation with a wise man is better than ten years of study." **Chinese Proverb**

It is said that success is like a combination safe---once you get the combination right, the safe will open. The simplest way to get it opened is to ask those who know the combination. I have learned that if you want to achieve success easier or quicker and with less pain, then study how other successful people did it and then simply ...copy them!

You may have heard the statement that experience is the best teacher. The truth is *other people's experience is the best teacher.* It allows you and I to advance faster because they have shared these experiences. In this book, I provide the opportunity to learn from some of the wisest, "richest" people from whom I have had the pleasure of learning. You will not want to miss a single lesson. It's like having a conversation with some of the greatest minds of all time...

This ULTIMATE GUIDE will assist you in taking all that your teachers and professors have taught you and multiplying it's effectiveness through "real world" lessons and wisdom. I sprinkle in some *"Uncle Dave"* advice in hopes of making your journey a little smoother and more enjoyable. I hope you will keep this book handy, referring back to it often as a source of guidance, reference and inspiration.

GROWING PEOPLE

If your vision is for a year, grow wheat.
If your vision is for ten years, grow trees.
If your vision is for a lifetime, grow people.
Chinese proverb

For more than twenty years, I have been in the business of people development---growing people through my varied endeavors both in the business world and in academia. I like helping people grow-challenging them to stretch-to go inside them themselves and find the resolve to make things happen.

As Eleanor Roosevelt stated above to *"taste—experience to the utmost, and reach out for newer and richer experiences."*

Like many of you, I was the first in my family to graduate from college. Often, it was a struggle overcoming numerous obstacles just to get that diploma. Allow me to join the many educators, counselors, professors, parents and mentors who have guided, supported, and challenged you, and applaud your accomplishments.

They believe that you have what it takes to compete in this world. They have done their best to prepare and encourage you, so now they can only hope that you will use all that you have learned and go out and see just how far you can go!

I am certain that these valuable, time tested lessons will be of help to you as you strive to fulfill your destiny...that dream that lives within you...that magical "someday" life that awaits your arrival.

Just know that you and *only* you can choose that destiny. It will be shaped one step, one action, one attitude and one relationship at a time. Day by day in every way, you decide when, where and with whom you share your future.

So, choose wisely. Dream BIG. And *NEVER, NEVER, NEVER* let anyone or anything keep you from your dream.

ENJOY THE JOURNEY...
WE ARE ALL ROOTIN' FOR YOU!!!

"A teacher affects eternity. (S)He can never tell where his (her) influence stops." **Henry Brooks Adams**

*"Far and away in the sunshine
are my highest inspirations.
I may not reach them, but
I can look up and see the beauty,
believe in them and try to
follow where they may lead."*

~Louisa May Alcott~

CAREER OF DREAMS
Oh, The Places You'll Go

*"I want to take my hat off to you young people
and say DREAM! Remember, one person
can make a difference."*
Archbishop Desmond Tutu

Welcome to the rest of your life. This is a special time for you as you prepare with great anticipation to continue on your success journey. There is always anxiety when we face the unknown. I encourage you to be confident, be strong, and be filled with great expectations as you seek to take the next step, a Big Step into your future.

Your imagination controls your future. If you want a highly successful future, you must nourish your imagination. As you think about your career, *AIM HIGH*. You have a lot going for you. There's a whole big world out there waiting for you to explore-so much to see-so much to do. And, yes, time is on your side. So, aim higher and you will go farther. Leave your limitations behind and let's begin the journey.

DREAM BIG

Dream as if we had forever....
Live as if this was the only day.

Everybody has a dream. A fantasy, if you like. It is the place where our highest inspirations and aspirations live. Usually such a dream takes the form of something that we would like to have, or do or to have happen to us.

How we respond to this dream determines whether or not we are successful. We may continue to dream and say: "If only I could ....", accepting that we will never see our dream come true. In this case our dream becomes a substitute for action. Or we can act on our dream, allowing *it* to become the model for our actions.

Kenny Chesney was born in Luttrel, Tennessee. Population: 915. A mere one thousand copies were made of his first album, which Chesney sold at his gigs, using the money to help buy a new Martin guitar. After graduating from college, Kenny headed to Nashville, where he performed everywhere he could, including an obscure place called HounDogs.

From those humble beginnings, Kenny has gone on to huge success. His albums have gone platinum more than twenty times and sold over thirty million copies. Here's Kenny's take on having a dream:

"I started out as the guy playing for tips in college, with nothing but a dream and acoustic guitar. I refused to believe I couldn't...I would't give up. I just kept looking forward, seeing what else I could do and finding people who would dream along with me. You know, I think that is a lot of it, too, that willingness to keep dreaming no matter what anyone tells you."

What are your dreams? Perhaps you want to be a millionaire, own a nice home in the country, to drive a sports car, or to save the world. To many people, a dream is just some wild illusion. The fact is that you move your dream from a mere fantasy to your roadmap for a successful life when you take the following three steps:

1. Make a plan
2. Write it down
3. Take action

Commit to it--Buy into it--Make it yours. Never give up until you are living your dream. Do whatever it takes, as long as it is legal and ethical. You can accomplish anything in life you want...if you know what you want to do and where you want to go.

Do you remember in *Alice in Wonderland,* Alice asked the cat, "Would you tell me, please, which way I ought to go from here?" The cat answered, "That depends a great deal on where you want to go." Alice said, "Oh, I don't much care." The cat replied, "Then it really doesn't matter which way you go."

Which way do you desire your life to go? What is it that you want to do and be while you are here on earth? Your desires are the roadmaps to your future.

YOUR DREAMS ENERGIZE YOUR CAREER

There is, indeed, power in what we desire. When we move emotionally from something we *want* to something we *need*, a whole set of unforeseen powers emerge to bring these desires to fruition.

Once you know what you truly desire for your life, you must then imagine what life will be like when you fulfill that desire. If you want to be a millionaire, think of how you would spend your time, and the luxuries you would enjoy. If your life's purpose is to work with underprivileged people, envision the looks on their faces as you tend to their needs. Imagine the satisfaction you will feel, as your head hits the pillow after another challenging, fulfilling day.

When there is a burning desire, the whole person; body, mind and spirit moves forcefully toward bringing that desire to rest.

Try this simple, yet powerful exercise. Buy a notebook and write what your perfect day will be like when you've reached your defined goal or desire. Describe it in detail, jotting down *everything* that you would like to do. Be explicit: write it all out as vividly as you possibly can. When you have finished, read it back to yourself. What does it do to you? Can you feel yourself aching to live life that way? Does it make you feel a little jealous of those who enjoy that sort of life? If it does, well done. You have just created desire. If you've done it well enough, you should want that life so much that it hurts!

Read your notebook every day. Add more to it as you think of other things you would like to do. Your book will motivate you through desire. It will remind you of the reward waiting for you - and will inspire you to succeed.

MAKE IT REAL

To make your dream really come alive within you, you must create a multi-sensory experience. See it, touch it feel it, smell it! If you know which sort of car you would buy, go by the showroom and sit in it...test drive it...smell the leather ...hear the sound system. *"Let's see, where do I plug in my iPod?"* Find out about it. Get the specifics. How much does it costs? What extras are available? Get a brochure. Choose your colors. As you convert your dream into hard facts, you are creating a specific destination.

By doing this, you take a bold step toward achieving your dream. You begin to transition from being a thinker to a becoming a doer.

Positive action is vital to becoming a success. This creates a strong emotional connection between you and the goal you wish to attain. Your brain, your entire nervous system is absorbing the feelings you experience as you sit in your *dream machine*. You will be able to refer back to this connection as you go out and strive to bring your dream—your wish—your desire, to reality!

Dreams come in all sizes. Make sure they are appropriate for the efforts required to reach your goals. Start with something small like a pizza party, a new cell phone. Or, maybe, a new suit, new shoes, new Nikes.

Medium goal equals medium reward: perhaps take some friends out to dinner...take a weekend get-away in the mountains or at the beach. Then, later as your goals grow, so will your wishes and dreams. Bigger dreams might be a trip to Vegas, a *HOT* new sports car, a new home...you name it. If you dedicate yourself to the process of goal setting and goal getting, you will find that ANYTHING AND EVERYTHING IS POSSIBLE.

DELAY THAT IMPULSE

Now, here is a good place to warn you of an essential key to money management and dream getting. It's called delayed gratification. Sure, you *could* whip out a credit card and buy that amazing outfit. "I mean, it looks *so* good... I can wear it on an interview and increase my chances of getting that job." Hold on, now. We can justify anything, can't we?

In order for that dream or desire to be a powerful incentive for you, it needs to be delayed. You want to bring this dream to the forefront of your mind and then attach it to a plan of action. Otherwise, it has no power. Instead of being a reward that you earned, it's just another case of immediate gratification.

Here's the proof. Scientists in the emerging field of neuroscience explain the hot button of our brain. Deep in the center of our brain, level with the top of our ears, lies a small, almond-shaped knob of tissue called the amygdala (you knew that). We actually have two amygdalas, one on either side of our brain. This tiny built-in neuron equips us with a biological reactor that is more aroused when we anticipate reward than when we actually receive it.

When a person is in pursuit of something that they deem important to them, they generally are in a better place physiologically. So, by keeping your dream or aspiration in front of you, and delaying it until you earn it, you receive *more* value from the goal-setting, dream getting process.

That, in a nutshell (no pun intended) is how the super successful achieve such a state. They use their hearts' desires to keep them focused and motivated to perform. Meanwhile, the not-so-successful, often broke people, use it as something to just go out and get.

> *"Spectacular achievement is always preceded by spectacular preparation."* **Robert Schuller**

WHAT DO YOU EXPECT?

Experts on motivation disagree on a lot of things, but one thing they all agree on is that your levels of motivation are directly tied to your expected probabilities of success. If you believe you can do something (the goals are realistic), you are highly motivated. If, however, you think you can't (if goals are unrealistic) your motivation level falls off in a hurry.

The lesson here is to dream big dreams, but realize that the short-term goals that take you to the next plateau are the real keys to success.

Everyone sets goals. Some people set them on their own, while others have them set for them. Some make elaborate game plans for goal achievement, writing them down in their day planner while others cut out a picture from a magazine depicting something they *wish* they had, and stick it on their fridge or in a book. It might be a car, a house, a dream vacation, or power shopping.

Did you ever set a goal you failed to achieve? Ever stop in the middle of a goal? Ever fall back to your old ways? Everyone has. Want to know why? Most people set goals that are *way* over their heads... unrealistic. I'm all for stretching to reach meaningful goals. Yet, it's a proven fact that if your goals are so lofty that they are, in your mind, impossible, then you've only got two chances of reaching them...slim and none. So, instead of these goals motivating you, they are burying you. You get paralyzed by the realization that *they ain't happenin'*. Know what I mean?

Remember this little piece of advice from your Uncle Dave: "Inch by inch, anything's a cinch. Yard by yard, It's hard." Simple enough. I like to keep it simple.

That's the best advice I can give you when it comes to setting goals. That's why I created the STAIRS to Your Goals and Dreams. It's just putting one foot in front of the other. And the best part is that you get to decide how long you spend on each step, *and* how many times you climb the stairs to your next goal.

To have a career of dreams, we must create a habit of setting, and getting, goals. Goals are simply dreams with a date on them. Think of this process as your GPS--- Your Goal Positioning System! You must identify where you want to go, lock it in, and get going.

Set your goals with care.
They set the upper limits for what you expect
to get out of your life.
~Uncle Dave~

15

Let's Climb the Stairs to Your Goals and Dreams

"The elevator is broken.
We must take the stairs to success."
~Uncle Dave~

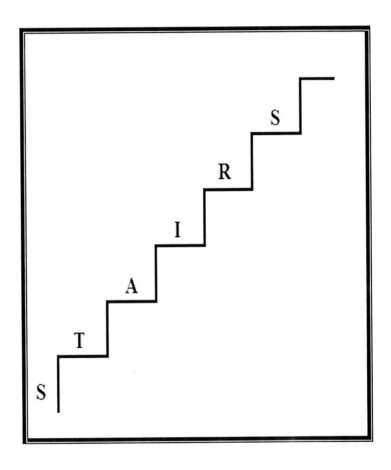

S STATE YOUR GOAL

The Two Cardinal Rules of Goal Setting are:

➤ **Write them down**

➤ **Be Specific**

Try something like this:

My goal is to have a position in the _____ field.

Or,

My goal is to work for _____ in the
_____department doing _____job.

      Take some time here. Put some serious thought into it. The more time you invest at the front end of the process, the more *real* it will become as a life-long habit of great reward. First, let the goal of what you want just flow. Then, refine it. Is this *exactly* the way that I want this to play out? Can I be more specific? S-T-R-E-T-C-H yourself. It's key that the goal is not only realistic, but is challenging, as well. If it's one, but not the other, it is not a good goal. In other words, if it's realistic, but easy, then it's a done deal. Not really a goal...more of a statement.

      For example: "I'm going to start my job May 30th, at XYZ Healthcare," when you've already got the job. You're really just stating a fact. That's cheating ...no fair. Realistic? Yes... Challenging? No. Just as: "I'm going to become president of Microsoft one week after graduation" is not a good goal.--- Why not?--Well, it's certainly challenging, *but* not all that realistic. I'm not saying you can't be president of Microsoft someday. It's just that the timeline might be a bit aggressive.

T TIMELINE

When do you want to reach this goal?

"I will begin my new position by August 10, 2XXX." There will be times when, due to circumstances, your goal is not reached on that precise day. It has happened to me a thousand times. Just re-set the goal and you stay on track. It may be off by a day, week, month or more. This does not mean the goal is not valid or reachable. It just means we did not put a proper timeline on it.

Sometimes, we reach the goal early. In which case, we just accept it, and move on...happily, for sure.

A ATTITUDE

Often, failure to reach our goals is caused by our underlying attitude. Do we believe it? Do we mean it? Did you really, truly *believe* that you could become Microsoft's president in a week? ...Maybe not.

"I will land this job because I qualify for the position due to my education, my community service and the internship I've done. In addition, I have part time training from my summer job. Most of all, I will provide the organization with a willingness to learn, serve and develop into the finest young _____ they have ever seen. I will over-deliver and prove myself worthy of the trust they have shown by hiring me."

By attitude, I do not mean a wild, unrealistic fantasy. What *is* meant is a spirit of can-do optimism--a strong conviction to make good things happen. With a firm resolve, you can make anything happen. Check your attitude. Do you *really* believe in your goal? Is this something that you really want? Once you have settled this, we can move on to the defining moment of goal setting, which is...

I INTENTIONS

When it comes to success in reaching our goals, it's really not what we say we'll do. It comes right down to what we truly *intend* to do. Put the power of intention to work focusing on what is best for you and having a clear plan of how you are going to achieve it. Then, once you have an objective and a strategy, take action!

Write your goals down, commit them to memory and then read them twice...three times every day. Don't put them away until you've achieved them. If it truly is *that* important to reach this goal, then your intentions must not only be *known* to you, they must be firmly believed by you, imbedded in you, and carried out by you.

Spending the time to write a step-by-step plan for its achievement is vital. In other words, what *action* do you intend to take to make the goal yours? Show me your written plan of attack. Who are you going to call?

This is the moment of truth for most. By investing the time, we make it real. We internalize it. We buy into it, and refine it...or discard it, realizing that no, this is *not* what I *really* want. It's trial and error...a process of elimination. It's our own *reality check*. It is the difference between the achievers and those who "almost made it"; between good and *spectacular* accomplishments.

Goals and intentions are linked. Intentions are the precursor to goal getting. Often, we say we want to do something or accomplish something, but we aren't really sold out on doing what it takes to achieve these things.

If our true intentions are not in line with what we are saying, then we are really not goal setting, just fantasizing. It's more like *Well if the stars all align...and the moon is in the seventh house...and all the lights are green, then I'll have a clear path to the place where I will buy that magical lottery ticket...I'll scratch it, and poof... out pops the genie-and hands me ten million dollars."*

WHAT ARE YOU GOING TO DO ABOUT IT?

You may have a goal, but it's your intentions that will dictate the outcome of your effort (or lack of?). *Why is this goal important? Is it money? Career advancement?*

What you intend to do are the key thoughts behind your actions. It's the action behind your thoughts that's the critical follow through. Just as in golf, your follow through determines where we go next... right? Instead of writing down your goals by themselves, a better exercise would be to write them with an attached intention statement. For example, *My goal is to get three job offers by July 16th.* In order to reach this goal, you will need to create a little to-do list for yourself. Like this:

I intend to:

- Update my resumé by Saturday.
- Network with two people a day from my circle of contacts...i.e. family, friends, present employer, professors, advisors, online social network, others.
- Take initiative to gain more knowledge about the position I wish to land. I will go to the website of the company or organization. I will read an article in a trade journal or online news source on the industry/field I am looking to go into.
- Associate with like-minded people; my mastermind group. Spend time with others who are looking to land a job, too. This is not social time. We shall compare ideas and resources to learn from one other.
- Other_____. You might leave one or two spaces blank, leaving room for your subconscious mind to help you find the plan, and the steps needed to reach your goal. When these new concepts come, add them to the list and act on them.

TOTAL COMMITMENT

For the STAIRS to take you to your goals and dreams, you *must* buy into your stated intentions. Here's what to do:

- **Date your list**
- **Print it out**
- **Sign it**
- **Make it Happen**

Carry it with you and follow it to the letter until each of the items you listed are complete. Don't end your day until you have, as you stated, contacted or networked with two people that day. Remember, this is not a social call, but a connection with the specific intent of asking them if they might know of someone who is looking to hire in the field you are seeking employment. If you're unclear as to what you need to do, ask your mentor, "What do I need to do to reach this goal? I know I need to read more, or call more, but what else do you see?"

Think of it in terms of taking a road trip. If you know where you want to go, but continually take actions which move you farther from your destination, you will never get there. The easiest trips occur when you know where you're going, and move directly towards your goal.

Create the intention and then take all the steps you can think of to align your actions with that intention. If you do not follow through on your intentions, either:

1. The goal was not really that important.
2. You lost focus or got distracted.

In either case, you must re-set the goal, re-commit to it, and redefine your intentions. Otherwise, abandon that goal and move on to a goal you *really* want and repeat the process.

CAUTION: Do not use this as a cop-out on your goals. The more clearly you define your intentions, the less abandoning of goals will be necessary.

Take time on each of these steps to become a goal-getting machine! Remember, GPS...

R REWARD—THE DREAM...

Congratulations, you did it! Whatever your goal was, you deserve a reward for accomplishing it. Think of it as a personal trophy for winning. Each goal needs to have an appropriate reward attached to it; the bigger the goal, the bigger the reward.

Don't skip this step (like I used to). What happens is, the subconscious, if you have conditioned it, will strive to steer you toward the goal, expecting the reward. If you default on the reward, then you take the power out of the process. So, there's no need to perform.

See the rewards small, medium and large: go to a concert, a weekend get-away, a new suit, new cell phone, new car, go to Europe, to own a home. Just make the reward fit the effort... and make it meaningful.

"Years from now you will be more disappointed by things you didn't do than by the ones you did do. So throw off the bowlines. Sail away from the safe harbor.

Catch the trade winds in your sails. Explore. Dream. Discover. You can't depend on your eyes when your imagination is out of focus." **Mark Twain**

S SET NEW GOALS—WHAT'S NEXT?

So, what's next? As you prepare to climb the stairs again, know that you can have several goals at once. They might be in different parts of your life. Say, one in the professional area, another in your personal life, financial, spiritual, health, and so forth.

For each goal you set, you will need to apply it to the STAIRS process. State it properly, define the timeline, check your true attitude toward it, declare your intentions, and ultimately, claim your reward. Be sure to write down your plan of attack with dates to measure your progress. Then strap on your helmet, stay focused, overcome the obstacles as they come along. And persist...Never give up... Keep getting up...until you reach *your* dreams...

Remember this; you are the author of your autobiography. If you want a better life, write a better script. No one can do that for you. You must decide why you really *do* want a better life...the dream...*your* dream.

Okay, let's have some fun. Give your left brain a rest, and let's engage that right amygdala. Here's a list of possible dreams, including places to go...things to do, to have... to experience. Just for kicks, pick three or four that you'd like to do...Ready....

Things To Do While I'm Alive

- Scuba dive in the British Virgin Islands
- Climb the Great Wall of China
- Write a book
- Drive on The Autobahn
- Celebrate Mardi Gras in New Orleans
- Attend a luau in Hawaii
- Tour The Greek Islands on a private yacht
- Go to The Super Bowl
- Play in The Swiss Alps
- See The America's Cup in Australia
- Fly a plane or helicopter
- Golf the top ten courses in the world
- Travel Route 66 in a convertible or Harley
- See the Aurora Borealis
- Cure a disease
- Drive a race car
- Parasail
- Go to The World Series
- Explore Europe by train
- Swim with the dolphins
- Sponsor a scholarship fund
- Helicopter ski in British Columbia
- Experience peace, love and joy

That's a good start. I am sure some of you have many more dreams you can add to your list. By all means, do it. It gives you something exciting to shoot for. And, believe me, it will make going to work some days worthwhile, because you are not working for a paycheck, you are chasing your dreams...

CAN YOU SEE IT?

I firmly believe that if you really want to achieve any dream, you can. It's a decision. *"I want to do it. I WILL do it, whatever it takes to reach the goal and live the dream."* The more clearly and precisely you describe your dreams—visualizing them--turning them into clear targets, the easier it is to focus on the means for their attainment. Eleanor Roosevelt said: "The future belongs to those who believe in the beauty of their dreams."

I say: *Never* let anybody steal your dream!

BEWARE OF THE DREAM SNATCHERS

They are out there everywhere, disguised as a friend, sometimes even family members. Unsure that they can live their dreams, they want you to keep them company in mediocrity. Don't fall for that. You'll wish you hadn't. When they come knocking, remember I told you so. I give you permission to close the door on such negative vibes, and press on with your BIG dreams.

I was contemplating starting my own business, so I called a friend to come by and listen to my potential partner and his concept. Jay was someone I considered pretty successful, so I valued his opinion. As soon as the presentation was finished, Jay got up, and he said to me: "Good luck to you. It looks like you want to grab for the brass ring called your dreams." And with that, Jay left.

You know, that was more than twenty years ago, and I have not seen Jay since. Yet, that night, I had a decision to make. Was I going to let Jay's snide remark decide for me if I could reach for my dreams? Or, would I take a risk of failing, and go for them?

I made a decision to trust my gut and not let Jay steal my dreams. That business grew to become a *twenty million dollar* success for us, and ultimately providing my family with financial independence and a life of uncommon freedom.

Sorry, Jay, I have no regrets. Chasing a dream is always better than going through life wondering about what could have been. Had I listened to him, I might still be working for someone else, never realizing my full potential as a dedicated people builder.

LET NOBODY STEAL YOUR DREAM--PERIOD

Your life can and *will* be much richer if you DREAM BIG. Besides, men and women who are chasing their dreams are living a more joyful and fulfilling life than those who just watch TV and go to bed bored.

Pursuing a goal is a constantly evolving process. No one who has ever followed a dream has taken a direct, unobstructed path and arrived at his or her destination. Following a dream is not a direct highway, but a bumpy road   full of twists and turns and occasion al roadblocks. The journey requires modifications and adjustments in both thought and action, not just once, but over and over. And that means you must be flexible and creative.

Mostly, you must be committed...really committed to do whatever it takes. Without that full commitment, you will turn away when the first obstacle comes along. There are two ways to look at an obstacle. It can be a stumbling block, one that trips you up and stops you from reaching your goal and ultimate dream.

Or, you can see that obstacle as a stepping stone, one that, when you look back at the journey, you identify it as the place where you briefly stopped. This stop was where you were required to rethink your mission. It forced you to look inside and decide, "Is this something I *really* want, or is it just a daydream? Are my intentions aligned with my goal, or is it time to abandon my dream?"

THE POWER OF A DREAM

Regina Spector Born in Russia, Regina was nine years old when her family decided to leave Russia to pursue their dream of coming to America They believed this was the land that promised a better life. To do this, however, Regina would have to abandon her cherished piano.

Regina had shown promises of brilliance whenever she sat at her piano. It was indeed her finest source of communicating her extraordinary, yet raw talent. Although she loved her piano, and her parents enjoyed hearing her make magic on the ebonies and ivories, their dream of a better life was even stronger.

As they began a new life in Brooklyn, New York, Regina discovered that she had not left her passion for the piano in Moscow. She found her fingers gliding along the windowsills and tabletop of their humble apartment, as *they* became her invisible piano.

Soon after settling in, they discovered there was a seldom-used piano in the basement of a nearby synagogue, and Regina was reunited with her one true love. Regina tells the story of a tiny stage in that basement. She would go up on that stage and, while holding an imaginary microphone, she would pull back the curtain announcing (to the invisible audience):---*"Introducing Piano Soloist Ms Regina Spector...!"* She envisioned herself sitting down and performing beautifully, then hearing the hearty applause, she took a bow to the appreciative and adoring audience.

This is how Regina Spector kept her dream alive. Her ability to do so when so many others would have abandoned theirs, has given the world this amazing talent. Regina has performed on television networks across the United States and Europe, and regularly tours worldwide.

What could you and I share with such a world-class talent? We, too, have dreams and goals, and face obstacles that can get in the way of reaching them. It is our choice whether we move past the temporary setbacks, or use them as the excuse that stops us from being all that we can be. So, don't give up. Don't quit. Don't be one of those poor souls who die with the music still in them.

In closing this very important first chapter, I will ask you to remember these facts:

- If your dream is bigger than you're obstacles, you will find a way to overcome.

- The difference between your present and your future is the self-portrait that you hold in your mind.

- It's not what happens to you along the road to success, it's how you handle it that determines whether you reach your goals and live your dreams...or not.

- Persistence and determination win out every time.

- It's not so much what we "get" from the pursuit of our dreams, as what we become in the process.

- Those who are in a constant state of pursuit, of achieving, of making a difference *always* get more than they bargained for.

Define your goals. Take the stairs to a life of great accomplishment and fulfillment. And most of all...

NEVER GIVE UP ON *YOUR* DREAM

Here is where you can refine your life's direction:

❖ Define one goal to put through the Stairs to Your Goals and Dreams process.

❖ What obstacle holds you back from creating and committing to your dream?

❖ What are you going to do to overcome that obstacle?

❖ If time nor money were an object, what dream or ambition would you like to accomplish?

❖ Who else gets to contribute and participate in your dream?

❖ Where do you see yourself in five years? Ten years?

Possibility Thinkers Creed

When faced with a mountain,
I will not quit!
I will keep on striving
until I climb over,
Find a pass through,
tunnel underneath,
Or simply stay and
turn the mountain
into a gold mine ---
With God's help!

Dr. Robert Schuller
Founding Pastor
Crystal Cathederal Ministries

ATTITUDE
Makes the Difference

"The greatest discovery of my generation is   that
people can alter their lives by altering their attitudes
of mind."
William James, from *As a Man Thinketh*

ATTITUDE: DOES IT MATTER?

Richard Bolles in *What Color is your Parachute?* states that attitude is the *NUMBER ONE ATTRIBUTE* that potential employers look for when interviewing a candi date for a position.

Beyond a doubt, the most important change I had to make to become a success was to change my attitude. Now, granted, this was not something I learned playing ball in the project. They did not offer-- "Get Your Attitude Out of The Gutter 101" where I went to school. I embarked on a journey of personal and professional development about seven years after graduation. And when I did, my income quadrupled, my self worth soared and my "Happiness Barometer" went off the charts!

It was a revelation that *I* was in charge of my own attitude. *I* controlled how *I* viewed life. *I* decided how things affected me, positively or negatively. My outlook on life was a decision. Wow! That was HUGE!

Up until that time, I was a victim of circumstances, or so I believed. I wasn't born rich. My parents were split. I didn't even know my dad (still don't), and I was living in the project. So, what can I do? Not much. Well, if anyone needed a check up from the neck up, it was me. I was a walking, talking bad attitude with a chip on his shoulders.

Through a professional contact, I was introduced to a classic book called *Think and Grow Rich* by Napoleon Hill. And that book changed my life. While attending law school at Georgetown, Hill was given access to some 500 of America's wealthiest and most influential people, the likes of which included Thomas Edison, Henry Ford, Andrew Carnegie and many more. He spent twenty years of his life studying their principles of success. This book, which I highly recommend, captured the world's first philosophy on personal achievement. It is truly a treasure for the ages.

I became a dedicated self-developer, and I encourage you to do the same. It was the constant powerful input from a wide array of positive sources, fortified by the fact that these were principles from the most successful people in all fields, that transformed my life. Some would call it brainwashing. Well, I must confess that my brain sure needed a good washing…a thorough scrubbing has done me a world of good.

Successful author James Malinchak says "You can't make millions with a poverty-conscious mindset." And how successful is Oprah Winfrey? I mean she has got one of the most successful talk shows ever. She has opened schools in Africa, and gives support to numerous great causes and is a beacon of hope for so many. Here's what she says about believing in yourself:

"The man who believes he can do something is probably right, and so is the man who believes he can't. I don't think of myself as a poor deprived ghetto girl who made

good. I knew from an early age I was responsible for myself, and I had to make good."

They are so right. Just as James and Oprah said, I had to overcome my "project mentality" to have a fighting chance of being financially successful. Such a mentality is very limiting. You feel inadequate—second rate— and unworthy of accomplishing great things.

After all, the internal story goes, *"I'm just a kid from the project. Who am I to think I can make something of my-self? No one else from the project does."* I had to *believe* that I was worthy. I had to accept responsibility for my own success. I had to decide to get better, to adjust my attitude. I was the one who had to believe that I *could* make something of myself. And so do you.

Growing up, we all have limiting attitudes. You may not have a project mentality--but a variation on the theme. I have heard it called a mill-town mentality, bayou mentality, broken family mentality, immigrant mentality, and even rich kid mentality. Whatever you call it, whatever you've got, let me offer up some simple, straightforward advice to you. Are you ready for it? Are you sure? Here it comes---A drum roll please! GET OVER IT……..PERIOD.

To move on and move up in life, you need to let go of the shackles of a bad attitude. The poor me syndrome won't cut it in the real world. The baggage of the past will only keep you down. Get yourself a new attitude. Begin to think positive. Speak positive. Be positive. Most importantly, ACT positive. Change what you do and how you do it and begin to steer yourself in a better direction.

American psychologist Dr. William Glasser said:

"If you want to change your attitude, start with a change in behavior. Begin to act the part, as well as you can, of the person you would rather be, the person you most want

to become. Gradually, the old, fearful person will fade away."

Believe that you *can* make it. Believe that you *will* succeed. Believe that anything is possible if you work hard enough, continue to grow, seek advice from wise sources and, most of all....NEVER, NEVER, QUIT!

Olivia Goldsmith is a shining example of belief. In trying to sell her manuscript, *First Wives Club,* she was turned down for *three years* by every major publishing house and studio. It went on to become a best-selling book and a HUGE box office hit. Olivia said: *"My experience taught me a valuable lesson. As long as you believe in yourself and your own vision, you have something. When you give up that, you are personally bankrupt."*

YOU GOTTA BELIEVE FOR YOU TO ACHIEVE

Be positive. Walk it. Talk it. Eat it. Drink it. Dress it. Be it. Like a great actor or actress, if you want the world to come to know and understand and love the person you are portraying, you must "put that person on." Pour that person you want to be *into* you, and you will *become* that person.

Life is a gift. Open it up each day and be thankful.

"No pessimist ever discovered the secrets of the stars, or sailed to an uncharted land, or opened a new heaven to the human spirit." **Helen Keller**

HAVE AN ATTITUDE OF GRATITUDE

Author Melody Beattie said: "Gratitude unlocks the fullness of life. It turns what we have into enough… a meal into a feast, a house into a home, a stranger into a friend. Gratitude makes sense of our past, brings peace for today, and creates a vision for tomorrow."

The difference between a prison and a monastery is just the difference between griping and gratitude. Gratitude is the opposite of entitlement. In my teaching and speaking to students, I often encounter the attitude of: *"Hey, world, what are you going to do for me?"* My reply is one that I have learned from being out in the real world for a good while now. It's short, sweet and to the point:

The world owes you nothing.

Regardless of your upbringing, or country of origin, race, or religion, if you expect the world to stop and hand it all to you, you are in for a big surprise. The only thing that we are entitled to is opportunity. The rest is up to us. So, it is in your best interest to be appreciative of any break or opportunity that you are presented.

> *"It is better to say thank you to a hand up than to believe you are entitled to a hand out."* **Uncle Dave**

We all have our down days: times when nothing seems to go right. Let's face it, it is easy to be "UP" when things are rolling smoothly. The true test of attitude is being "UP" even when you are "down." Hey, stuff happens. We cannot control all that happens to us. A secret of success is to handle the unpleasant things along the way, put them in perspective, and then the "Stuff" seems less important. An attitude of gratitude is the cornerstone of a happy life.

IF I COULD ONLY SEE

"The man who acquires the ability to take full possession of his own mind may take possession of anything to which he is justly entitled."
~Andrew Carnegie~

There was a young lady who hated herself because she was blind. She seemed to despise everyone, except for her loving boyfriend. Always there for her, she vowed that if she could only see, that she would marry him.

One day, someone donated a pair of eyes, allowing her to see for the first time. Overjoyed by his girlfriend's ability to see, he went to her, proposing:

"Now that you can see everything, my dear, will you take my hand in marriage, so that we can spend the rest of our lives together?"

Looking in his eyes for the first time and listening to his beautiful request, she discovered that he, too, was blind. As she gazed at her loving boyfriend, she gave her answer. "No," she replied. She would not marry him, as she "could not be married to a blind man."

Crushed by her rejection of his unconditional love, the young man turned away in tears. As he left her presence for the last time, he asked a friend to give her a simple note, stating: "My love, just take care of my eyes."

To those who witnessed this sad event, the message was clear---Though she had gained eyesight, her true heart had not changed.

What is your true outlook on life? Do you think like: *"Well, if I can just get an A in this class..."* Or, *"If I can just get a date with so and so, then life will be perfect."* I'm going to let you in on a little secret--Ready? Life will *never* be perfect. Money won't make it perfect, nor will the right mate, a fancy car or a big house. Our attitude is what makes it the way it is. Either we are always dissatisfied, or we appreciate all that life offers.

Think about these things:

- Today before you say an unkind word, think of someone who can't speak.
- Before you gripe and moan about how tough your courses are, give a thought about those who don't get the opportunity to earn a degree.
- Before you complain about the taste of your food, think of someone who has nothing to eat.
- Today before you complain about how hard life is, think of someone who went to heaven too young.
- Before whining about the distance you drive, think of someone who walks the same distance with their feet.
- Before pointing the finger at another, remember there are three more fingers pointing back at you.
- When depressing thoughts get you down, put a smile on your face and thank God you're alive and kickin'.

BEING POSITIVE IS GOOD FOR YOUR HEALTH

Positive thoughts can be as effective as drugs in beating diseases. Studies show that the negative thoughts that go through your head in a day have a more harmful effect than skipping veggies and feasting on junk food. You destroy yourself from the top down.

There is a growing body of evidence to suggest that a patient's beliefs and hopes affect their prognosis. A major contributor to maintaining health and removing disease is an attitude of the patient, says Professor Oakley Ray, a psychologist from Vanderbilt. He reviewed 100 years of research for a paper published in American Psychiatrist and concludes that words can have the same effect as drugs; thinking optimistically can change your whole biology.

Ray discovered a significant amount of evidence to support this, including various studies suggesting one's attitude may be linked to heart disease. He cites a study from The Harvard School of Public Health, which established that while optimism lowers risk of heart disease in older men, pessimism and hopelessness increase it. The evidence shows that patients with heart disease who feel hopeless about their condition have a longer recovery.

Dr. Robert Schuller calls it "Possibility Thinking". Schuller teaches that possibility thinkers succeed as they train themselves to look for the positive in all situations. They overcome second-rate thinking, and listen to new ideas with an open, "possibility" mindset. Through their commitment to "possibilitizing", such people become hope-boosters, confidence-creators, enthusiasm-generators ---dedicated dreamers.

They are great people to be around, as their exuberance for life is contagious. I am a dedicated "Possibility Thinker." I live by *The Possibility Thinkers Creed.* How about you? I find that people with a positive attitude and equally positive self-talk are significantly more successful, well-balanced and effective than those who go through life with a negative, self defeating attitude. Transform your attitude from negative to positive, and you'll realize your full potential. And you may even live longer!

ENTHUSIASM MAKES THE DIFFERENCE

Enthusiasm is contagious. Ever been around someone who is enthusiastic about what they are doing? You get a lift just being in the same space as them, don't you? A key element of a positive attitude is enthusiasm. Whether it's a new idea or project, a new relationship or teaming up on a meaningful endeavor, be enthusiastic about it and your effectiveness and your "infectiveness" will soar.

You will enjoy the experience and you'll attract others who do the same as they become positively infected with the excitement you exude for the project. To go to the top, you'll want to light that enthusiasm up! -- When you do, it becomes passion. And passion is *enthusiasm on fire!*

Donald Trump says: "Passion is the catalyst for great success. If you don't have passion, everything you do will fizzle out, or be mediocre, at best. It's an intangible momentum that can make you indomitable."

Light the fire within. Fan those flames of enthusiasm and drive your desires for success with PASSION.

"Every great and commanding movement in the annals of the world is the triumph of enthusiasm. Nothing great was ever achieved without it."
~Ralph Waldo Emerson ~

GET THE EDGE

Dr. Denis Waitley is a respected author, lecturer and consultant on high performance human achievement. He has studied and counseled winners in every field from Apollo astronauts and Super Bowl champions, to government leaders and youth groups. He has served on the U. S. Olympic Committee's Sports Medicine Council.

In *The Winner's Edge,* Dr. Waitley writes about the importance of attitude to achieve great success:

At the world-class level, talent is nearly equal.

- On the PGA tour, only a few strokes per year separate the top money winners from the rest of the players.

- In baseball, batting champions get only 20-30 more hits in an entire season than those below the top ten.

- In the Olympic, the difference between the gold medal winner in the 100 meter dash and the fourth place, non-medal winner is less than two-tenths of a second.

What's true in sports is also true in business and in life. There's but a fractional difference between winners in life and those who merely exist. The difference is attitude under pressure. It's the winner's edge.

Positive attitude has nothing to do with what happens to you. It's what you do with-how you react to what happens to you. A positive attitude comes from your ability to process thoughts in a positive way, regardless of circumstances, and it's never 100%. That's why, in spite of a determination to be positive at every moment, there will be highs and lows based on your thought process and your vulnerability to others. Here's the good news: The more you work on your attitude, the less vulnerable you become to the negative.

ATTITUDE IS A DECISION

"Be positive every single day. You must work at it daily, because no one else is going to do it for you."
~Uncle Dave~

Two little boys were put in separate rooms. The first boy's room was filled with all the newest toys--video games, action toys, things to ride, things to build and destroy. If you name it, it was in there.

The other boy's room was just a huge pile of manure. No colorful toys. No action heroes and, oh, can you imagine, *NO* video games? Just manure piled high and deep.

Each room had a one-way window, so people could observe. The first boy rifled through the various toys, tossing them aside, unappreciatively ranting and raving: *"There's nothing in here I want to play with."*

The other boy was having a great time. Tossing the manure up high, getting it all over himself, making excited screeching sounds.

After a few minutes of observation, they opened the door and asked the two boys how they were doing. The first boy continued to rant and show his displeasure. *"This is no fun. I want something good to play with."*

When they opened the second door, that boy was still tossing the manure around, jumping around in it, and generally, having a great time. When asked why he was having so much fun he replied *"With all this manure, I know there's a pony in here somewhere."*

Positive attitude has been preached since the writing of the Bible. Every major philosopher, every major theologian, and especially every major personal development expert has preached the virtue of positive thought, positive action, and positive attitude for centuries. Millions of works have been written on the subject.

You would think, with all this proof, that everyone (you included) would have a positive attitude. If you did, you would be wrong. You can read and listen all you want, but unless you *decide* to become a positive person-- one who thinks, acts, and speaks positive (both proactive and reactive) your attitude will not be a positive one.

Decide to be positive and stick with that decision. It *will* change your life. It has certainly changed mine.

PERSISTENCE

"We all have dreams. But in order to make dreams come into reality, it takes an awful lot of determination, dedication, self-discipline, and effort." **Jesse Owens**

41

After big success in *Butch Cassidy and the Sundance Kid,* and *The Way We Were,* Robert Redford was told "NO" for four years while trying to get "All The Presidents Men" produced. In spite of the combined star power of both he and Dustin Hoffman, the project still brought consistent rejection. Eventually he got that movie made because, as Redford said, his *"belief in the movie was stronger than their rejection."*

What a simple, powerful message! If we want to succeed, our belief must be stronger than any rejection. By the way, the movie went on to win four Oscars! When asked: *"What keeps pushing you?"* he reply: *"I believe if you can do more, you should."*

Already a superstar when he started the Sundance Film Festival, Redford tells of standing outside the theatre where the films would be aired and virtually "pushing" people in to watch the featured movies, twenty years later no one needs to be pushed into Sundance.

Since then, Sundance has become *the* place to be seen for all the "beautiful people" each November. In both of these examples, it was Robert Redford's attitude that propelled first his movies, then the festival, on to success. I mean, admit it, if you saw Robert Redford outside a theatre asking you to come in, you'd go wouldn't you? It would be hard to say no.

Yet, it was not because Redford's name was on them that created its success. It was his persistence and a willingness to put his ego aside and to serve others by literally ushering people into the theatre that made the difference.

The same holds true for the new grad. Sure, in some ways, you've "earned" your admission into the real world. You've worked hard, got good grades, put together a fine resume...all the right stuff. But like Robert Redford, even a "Magna Cum something" does not guarantee your success. You must develop that same persistent attitude that he had.

Go out and be willing to serve. If you serve, you deserve. It is not below us. To humble our selves is to put *our* egos in check and allow the flow of possibilities. In this fast paced, super-competitive twenty-first century, if we don't, someone else will. The world is a little better when someone is willing to put down their "entitled" self and chooses to stand outside a theatre and walk someone to their seat. That, my friends, is how you become a true star in this world.

> *"Success does not come overnight. It takes persistence to make it."*   **Uncle Dave**

EXPECT GREAT THINGS IN YOUR LIFE

"High expectations are the key to everything."
~ **Sam Walton**~

What do you expect? That's a big question. The American Heritage Dictionary defines Ex-pec-ta-tion:

- To look forward to the *probable* occurrence or appearance of someone or something; to consider *likely* or certain; to anticipate *confidently*. Let's take a look at these words...

If you approach every day expecting good things to *PROBABLY* happen, then what do you think will happen? Chances are good things are *LIKELY* to happen. We put the odds in our favor. Get excited about that! It's no guarantee everything will be just perfect. There is no such thing in the real world. Yet, more often than not, you get what you expect.

CONFIDENTLY. If we anticipate confidently, we are pretty sure of the way things will turn out. We have a good feeling about this. We *EXPECT* to win, right? I have discovered that it is much better to expect to win than to expect to lose. We walk taller, feel better, and look better when we carry an air of confidence. The world stands and takes notice. The universe cooperates. So, why not have *great* expectations for your future? Why not expect the odds are going to favor you? It is more *LIKELY* that they will when you believe they will, and when you walk with confidence everyday. Life, they say, is a self-fulfilling prophecy.

In *The Seven Habits of Highly Effective People,* Steven Covey advises: *"Have an abundance mindset, not a scarcity mindset."* What a terrific concept. Think about an abundant harvest. Envision a future filled with abundant joy and happiness... abundant fulfillment.

Employ the Law of Attraction. This law states that you attract to you in your life what it is that you put out into universe. If you put out doom and gloom, you'll attract the same. If you put out optimism and abundance, the universe returns optimism and abundance. Like a mirror, life tends to reflect back at you what you present it. So, if you don't like what you are attracting, you must change what you put out.

"Trust yourself. Create the kind of self that you will be happy to live with all your life. Make the most of yourself by fanning the tiny, inner spark of possibility into flames of achievement." **Foster C. McClellan**

A BAD ATTITUDE CAN SABOTAGE A CAREER

"The happiest people don't have the best of
everything. They just make the best of everything."
~Uncle Dave~

Jen, a graduate student working in a medical center, explains a situation at work: "Our manager recently hired another student, Andrew, to do work similar to mine. Now Andrew is trying to wiggle his way into my project. I don't know whether our manager is encouraging him to do this, but I don't like it. I am quite protective of this project, which is very high-profile.

I call Andrew the 'information stalker,' because he asks a million questions. As a private person, I find all of this intrusive. He has aligned himself with the 'Queen Bee' of the department, whom I personally despise.

Look, I just don't trust these people. I keep my distance and avoid communicating with them. However, I am starting to realize that this might make me seem difficult to work with, and Andrew could use that to his advantage. I need to guard against Andrew's devious ways, but I don't want to sabotage myself."

What's the real problem here? Or, should I say *who* is the real problem? It seems to me that *attitude,* in this case a guarded, defensive and difficult-to-work-with demeanor, is really what is wrong with this picture. Jen's putting her personal feelings ahead of getting the job done spells uncooperative. Combine that with a low tolerance for different work styles and yes, Jen, you probably *are* sabotaging yourself.

Rather than burning a lot of energy on political plotting and defending her turf, it would be in Jen's best interest to address her attitude toward these situations. Over the course of a long career, situations will so often arise when a positive, cooperative, tolerant attitude will win out for the benefit of all involved. Many bright, talented people self-destruct because they do not work well with others. If Jen continues down this path, she hurts her own career more than Andrew ever could.

> *"The bottom line, trash the pessimistic attitude."*
> **~Donald Trump~**

This all begins in our thoughts. How we think is how we live. There is a saying that goes: "Sow a thought, reap an action; sow an action, reap a habit; sow a habit, reap a character; sow a character, reap a destiny." Our thought patterns ultimately take us to our destination..

We become one thought at a time, a by-product of the way we think. Watch your thoughts closely and change the pattern if you don't like where it's headed. Don't let the circumstances control your thoughts. Don't let others determine how you think. You must take charge of how you think if you are to have any say in the way your life unfolds. You *can* control your destiny if you choose to think right.

I would encourage you to dress your mind each day when you dress your body. A success-minded person would not go out into the world half-dressed. Then, you shouldn't go out until you have dressed your mind with a dose of positive expectations. They will protect you from the negative forces you will encounter during the day and fortify your mind to keep you on track for a successful journey.

So, plant some positive seeds in your brain, and go out fully dressed to win.

It's time for your check-up from the neck up:

❖ Is your attitude in the right place to attract the best job or opportunity for advancement?

❖ What would you identify as your strength in the attitude department?

❖ Who do you look up to as a role model when it comes to a healthy attitude?

❖ Choose a favorite quote or affirmation to boost you when your attitude is challenged.

❖ How high are your expectations?

"Remind yourself regularly that you are better than you think you are.

Successful people are not super human. Success does not require a super-intellect.

Successful people are just ordinary folks who have developed belief in themselves and what they do.

Never - yes, never- sell yourself short."

~David Schwartz~

LESSON 103

SELF IMAGE
Who Do You Think You Are?

"No one can make you feel inferior without your consent." **Eleanor Roosevelt**

Are you comfortable with who you are? Will "who you are" fit in the work environment you aspire to join? If not, are you willing to grow? To change? Adapt? Not to be someone you aren't, but to present yourself in the best possible light to succeed in the environment you choose. How do I know what is required or expected? These are all valid questions. They are foremost in the minds of students preparing to enter the *real world.*

Self-esteem should be based on respect for yourself as well as a healthy, realistic appraisal of your abilities and talents. Yet too often it is based on a blind self-regard, à la Paris Hilton. Do not make the mistake of putting too much stock in the on-air persona of the "Beautiful People." Their actions are self-serving and do not work well in your efforts to build *your* self-esteem.

Growing up in the project, I was not surrounded by positive, uplifting thoughts and sayings. No one was writing encouraging messages on the sides of the buildings or on the sidewalks. There was plenty of *writing on the wall,* as it was, but none of it was inspiring. Nor were there many good role models. Sure, if you just wanted to steal cars or get into trouble with the law, there were plenty of "role models." But if you were looking for someone to follow to attain real success, you were best to look beyond the project. If you had that type of a childhood, then you face a special challenge increasing your self-confidence as an adult.

PROTECTING YOUR SELF ESTEEM

When you are seeking a job, your self-esteem will be challenged. When looking to successfully transition from academia to career, you most likely will experience a scary word. Now, this is not a word that we like to hear. We didn't like it as kids, nor as young adults. Now that you are armed with a degree, you certainly will not appreciate *anybody* using this word on you. Apparently, they just don't know who you are. They don't appreciate the fact that you and your family might have spent (invested) anywhere from $50,000 to over $250,000 on your education.

So, what is this word that's so bad? Brace yourself: Here it is... NO. That's the word. You might want to get familiar with it, even a bit comfortable with it, because in all likelihood, you will be hearing it, reading it and fearing it. Really, it's not a very big word, is it? Two little letters...NO.

Often, it comes with a reason (excuse?). No experience, not qualified, many applicants, position filled. Regardless of the reason, a NO is a NO is a NO, and it can really bruise one's self-esteem. Worse, it can cripple yours, if you allow them to.

Now, granted, I realize that you cannot control if someone answers your request for a job, or even an interview, with a NO. What you *can* control is how you handle this news. So, let's develop an approach to save your self-esteem, perhaps even build it up, during this most trying exercise called job-hunting.

YOUR JOB HUNTING REMEDY

The first thing we can do is to reduce the power that the NO has on us. Let's start by physically shrinking it down to size. From now on, it's no longer a NO...it's just a no. There, that was easy. You might think this is trivial, but it really isn't.

We have reduced its value as we have shrunk it down to size. The mere word should not affect us as much. Accept that, and we can move on. The truth is words only impact us to the degree that we put value...or power on them.

Next, realize that it's only a job. I know, I know, this *IS* important. It's your life, so you say. And you are right ... partly. It's just the beginning. For many, it is your very first job after getting all this formal education and preparation, so *"Now is NOT the time to fail. What if my friends get jobs and I don't? What a loser I'll be."* I disagree. There's no big red "L" on your forehead if you do not land a job before they do. Realize that you are NOT in competition with your friends or your fellow graduates this year. You are only in competition with you. That's right, only with yourself.

If we agree that you cannot control a prospective employer who says no, then you must move forward to work on something you *can* control. And, that something is Y-O-U. Proper perspective is vital, especially when it comes to your healthy self-image. So, how do we work on you. *Here's how:*

First -What is it that you REALLY want to do?
Why is this *"The One"?* Can you see yourself being happy in this career? Have you researched it thoroughly? This is a good time to go deep and answer the question: "Why have I chosen this job to go for?" Is it for the right reasons? "This is a career I'll enjoy, the type of people I relate to, or it's my kind of work?" Or, was it because "so

and so is going into it." Or, "I hear they have good benefits and it's close to home."

Any of these can be a good reason, but a one on one with yourself can be quite beneficial in determining if it is the best reason or the true reason for you.

Second -Are your objectives realistic?

Look at the position that you are seeking. Is this what you really want to do? Does it fit with your long-term objectives? Are you attempting to land the "dream job" right out of school, one that will last your whole professional life? I'm a firm believer in aiming high, yet when you are fresh out of school, getting your foot in the door is a realistic approach toward launching a successful career.

Third -Are you optimizing your search by using the right methods and tools ?

Contrary to public belief, posting a resumé on the Internet does not guarantee you will get hired. According to Richard Bolles in *What Color is your Parachute?* the Internet is the least efficient way to land a job...A mere four percent success rate.

Now, this does not mean to avoid it altogether. It DOES mean that you must seek additional sources to increase your chances of landing the RIGHT JOB. Mary Riley Dikel, creator of The Riley Guide, a directory of employment and career resources on the Internet, said: "The Internet is an absolutely necessary tool in your job search arsenal, but it's not your only tool, and if you're spending more than 15 minutes on the Internet, you're lost." See the Resources Section in the back of the book. Go to our website www.graduateandgrowrich.com for updates on best places for job-seekers to look.

Fourth -What's the worst that can happen if you don't land a job in this field?

There are other ways to get to your destination. Have you considered them? What are they? Identify three, and research the opportunities in these areas. Do you know anyone in this field to converse with?

Have a long-term perspective. This is just the beginning of your journey. I am of the opinion that things always work out the way they are supposed to work out. So, Even though it is difficult to see this when they're not going the way we want them to, or think they should go, when you look back with the benefit of 20/20 hindsight, you'll see why they happened a certain way. Trust it. Be positive. It will all work out for the best. Expect it.

Fifth- Make it Priority ONE

If after reviewing the first four remedies, you find yourself clear about what jobs you wish to pursue, then create a plan of action, and attack. Put aside things that take away from this priority. If you don't do this, then you're not serious about the search. It's not *that* important to you yet. But if it is, then you must *focus*.

Sixth-NEXT

If you get a no, move on. Network. Gather more information about your preferred field. Review your resumé. Be sure it speaks to the type person you seek an interview with. Get outside opinions. Someone you know who works in this field can provide invaluable insight. Speak with a career counselor. Do an online assessment.

Lastly, don't despair

You *will* get a job. Hopefully, it will be a perfect match on the first try. If not, use it as a learning experience, a stepping-stone along the way. But remember, what the job will bring to you is not nearly as important as what you bring to the job. Prepare yourself with a great attitude, you are miles ahead of most. And as you enter the workplace, seek to learn, to grow, to serve and you will be improving your self-esteem each and every day.

GROWING YOUR SELF ESTEEM

Most of the time, when a man or a woman look into the mirror they see the image that is in their mind of themselves, instead of what is reflected back in reality.

How do we get better? It begins with our habits. How we treat ourselves, talk to ourselves, act, associate with, and, in general, see ourselves. When it's one-on-one, us talking to us, what do we really believe about who we are, and how we fit into the world in which we live.

To grow our self-image, we must start with the belief that we *do* matter. We *do* belong. We are *truly* worthy. In his book *Real Magic,* Dr. Wayne Dyer said:

"Align yourself so the universal force of energy is something you can know intimately and use for life, even if no one around you knows what you are doing or believes in what you are talking about when you speak of miracles. Simply open yourself to a new inner belief system that says 'Maybe, just maybe, this is a possibility for me."

Joe was a detective in the Chicago area who worked with juvenile felons. He was plagued with the idea that no matter what he did to try to help these felons change their lives, they continued to resort to violence in the streets. Joe decided he would accept the possibility that by 1997 there would be a reduction in violent killings in Chicago. Though those working around Joe were quite cynical, Joe really believed it. He began to speak it into existence by discussing his ideas with influential people.

Joe believed this could be accomplished by helping teens change their internal belief systems about who they are, thus changing their self-image from the inside out. The combination of Joe's resolve and the assistance of others, helped Joe's dream come true, as they were able to significantly reduce violent crime against all odds. Joe's commitment to make a difference by helping people change the way they saw themselves confirms what Dr. Dyer claims.

He says: "Everyone who has ever come from a dirt-poor origin to create abundance has had to use the energy of God's potential within their minds before it could happen in the physical world... If miracle-working power is available to any impoverished soul, it is available to your impoverished soul should you decide that this is your truth."

Yes, it is. Believe you can be better, act on this belief, then one day at a time---one step at a time, you will improve your self-image, and, thus, open up the universe of possibilities to yourself.

TALK YOURSELF UP

"Happiness depends upon the quality of your thoughts."
~ **Marcus Aurelius   Roman Emperor**~

In his book *10 Seeds of Greatness,* Dr. Denis Waitley talks about the power of self-talk. He says: "You are your most important critic. There is no opinion so vitally important to your well being as the opinion you have of yourself. And the most important meetings, briefings and conversations you'll ever have are the conversations you will have with you."

We are all talking to ourselves every moment of our lives, except during a short portion of the sleep cycle. It comes automatically. We are not even aware that we are doing it. We have a non-stop commentary running in our heads.

Emerging research shows indelible links between what we are saying to ourselves and what we accomplish.

According to Dr. Pamela Butler, author of *Talking To Yourself,* "Your behavior, your feelings, your sense of self esteem and even your level of stress are influenced by your inner speech." Butler continues, "Everything we do is first created by our self-talk. Self talk shapes our inner attitudes, our attitudes shape our behavior, and, of course, our behavior, what we do, shapes our accomplishments."

So, if you tell yourself you are a winner, an achiever, then, for sure, you are much more likely to succeed than the person who talks themselves down.

Psychologist Shad Helmstetter, author of *What You Say When You Talk To Yourself,* states: "What we put into our brains is what we will get out." Garbage in--garbage out... positive in--positive out.

Thus, the number one rule for developing a healthy self-esteem is: *Say nice things to yourself.* Accept the fact that the most important opinion about you is the one that you hold. Ultimately, nobody else is responsible for your self-esteem. Nobody else is accountable for your actions but you. Therefore, nobody's opinion about you is more important than yours.

Make a habit of having daily conversations with yourself that are supportive and reinforcing. We appreciate when someone praises us, rewards us, or is happy to see us. Well, then, talk to yourself in the same respectful way and you will strengthen your self-esteem tremendously. It all begins right here, from the inside out.

HOW DO YOU TALK TO YOURSELF?

"We have found the enemy and it is us." **Pogo**

Do you ever catch yourself saying things like: *"Ugh, clumsy me. I messed up again."* Or, *"Wouldn't you know it, bad things always happen to me."* How about *"I can't do anything right."* Who's guilty of this?

I have good news! Researcher Gail Dusa says it's easy to change our self-talk. The key is "to reprogram our minds for success. We have a choice each time we think to be positive or negative." Many of us don't believe this, but it is true. We choose whether to program ourselves for positive, successful days, or negative downer days. It is a choice. And here's more good news. No matter how many times you have let circumstances ruin your day or set your attitude, it's never too late to decide to change that. Start today. Choose to speak highly to yourself.

For example, perhaps you catch yourself saying something like *"I'm always late,"* or *"I'm not good at remembering names."* Take action. Stop your inner talk and correct it. Replace those thoughts with *"No, I used to be late, but now I am on time."* And *"I am getting better with names everyday."* What we say is what we get; what we believe is what we become. The more you change your self-talk, the healthier self-esteem you build.

A great way to think about this process is what I call cut and splice. When they shoot TV shows and movies on film, they use this process.. They shoot hours and hours of footage and then edit it all down to the finished product. First, they cut out what they don't want, then the editor fast forward and splice in the next scene.

Well, you can use the same process. When a negative, derogatory message crosses the movie screen called your brain, just say, *"cut."* Then, imagine you are going to edit that out and say, *"splice."* You then can drop in the more positive, constructive message and be on your way. Practice this simple mental exercise. The more you use it, the less you'll have to edit. It takes time, but it is worth it. It worked for me!

We grow up in imperfect situations with mostly well meaning but imperfect parents, teachers trying to do their best in crowded classrooms, the influence of friends trying to find themselves, relatives who have their own problems and blemishes, and in neighborhoods that don't support becoming all that a person can become. Through it all, we develop limiting beliefs, attitudes, and habits of behaviors that severely limit what we can accomplish. Most people know that they have more to offer, yet many feel lost and unable to contribute like they would like to. All too often they resort to playing the victim and do not take responsibility for where they are in their lives.

Understand that you had little control of your life until now. Today is the moment of decision. The life you live today is a result of your choices in the past. The life you live tomorrow is a result of the decisions you make and actions you take today. Decide today that you need to let go of old beliefs and ineffective conditioning of the past by learning new things, developing new habits, and changing into a new person. Make little changes each day and over time you will make a huge difference in how you really feel about Y-O-U.

HOW DO YOU SEE YOURSELF?

"If you don't change your beliefs, your life will be like this forever. Is that good news?" **Dr. Robert Anthony**

There is an abundance of scientific evidence that shows an individual's mental picture of themselves, more than any other factor, sets the ultimate boundaries of their achievements. We now understand that our human brain acts like a high powered GPS and steers your life toward the realization of the mental self-image you feed it.

This law of self-image psychology, when implemented and reinforced, creates fundamental day-to-day behavior patterns, which become a self-fulfilling dream or nightmare, depending on the thoughts upon which it feasts. Control your thoughts…your self-talk, and you can control your destiny.

Self-belief is the fulcrum point of success. It's the bridge between personal attitude and enthusiasm, and your ability to transfer confidence to those who you might influence. If you believe it, you can achieve it... Period.

Napoleon Hill said: "Whatever the mind of man can conceive and believe, it can achieve." You *can* become a true person of power and positive influence. Often people put off this empowering belief, as they do not want to be perceived as having an inflated ego. Of course, some do have seemingly inflated egos. Usually, it is just overcompensation for a low of self-esteem deep inside of themselves. The majority of people do not really see themselves as they really are. We must believe our selves to be bigger and better than we have in our past.

Dr. Waitley states: "In my opinion, nothing's more important than your belief in your own potential for success and happiness, regardless of age, gender, ethnicity, looks, education or background. Self-confidence isn't something you're born with. It's something you develop."

You have the freedom to believe in your dreams and the opportunity to pursue your dreams with all your heart. It is your *beliefs* that drive your expectations. Expectations drive your *choices*. And, it is your choices that drive your *performance*.

Your performance ultimately delivers the *results* you expect, which leads directly to the *success* you desire. The long and short of it is this: Success *starts* with a strong *belief* in your ability to meet or exceed expectations. If you believe you can, you will. And, if you believe you can't, you won't.

**If you believe you CAN...Or you believe you CAN'T...
You're RIGHT!**

High expectations require tremendous belief. If you have little belief that you will achieve your goals, how much of your energy will you commit? If you believe your plans are doomed to failure anyway, how much effort will you expend in their pursuit?

If you lack strong belief in your team-building skills, or have little confidence in your organizational systems, will you have the attitude required to take the actions necessary to see your dreams through to completion? Negative beliefs limit your actions, which limits your future. Positive beliefs expand your actions, which expand your future.

NOBODY'S PERFECT AND THAT'S OKAY

I have come to realize that how I handled my mistakes in life had a direct impact on lowering or raising my self-esteem. If I dwell on those mistakes and beat myself up, I knocked myself down a notch, or two...or three.

How we treat ourselves is *the key component* in building and sustaining a positive self-image. Sure, we all mess up. We'll fall short, disappoint and fail. We must take all of this as a learning process. As we learn from our mistakes, we grow.

When I gave myself the benefit of the doubt, tried to learn from a personal misjudgment, I moved on and actually gained some self-esteem. Why? Because it took a lot of growth to accept that it was okay to mess up. Everyone does. I'm still "okay"...just human. And when you have a spell of self-doubt, remember *The Little Engine That Could.* Just keep repeating *"I think I can I think I can"* until that spell runs its course. And it will...It always will *IF* you keep believing in yourself. What was Whitney Houston's famous line? *"Learning to love yourself is the Greatest Love of all."*

Or try this; Just say FIDO. FIDO? What's that? I saw a man speak by the name of Clebe McLary. Clebe was a war hero. He had served his country in Vietnam. In the line of duty, he lost his arm, lost his buddies, nearly lost his life. Yet, there he was dressed in his military whites, decorated with an enormous amount of medals he earned for his courage, leadership and sacrifice.

During that talk, as he recalled so many incredible situations that occurred while serving, Clebe's iron will was always fortified with the saying FIDO-Forget It -- Drive On...So, whenever you hit a wall, whenever you are facing adversity or your self-image is being challenged, remember Clebe and just say FIDO--Forget It-- Drive On.

The American Psychological Association report that reaching for sky-high standards does not make people anxious and stressed out. Troubles begin when a persons self worth hinges on perfection. Those most invested in appearing perfect set themselves up for shame and inferiority, which, according to Gordon Flett of York University "fuels shame, depression and stress."

EIGHT STEPS TO A HEALTHY SELF IMAGE

These eight steps will prepare you for a life-long journey of abundance. A strong self-image improves how you feel about yourself, add value to all of your loved ones and increase the enjoyment of your life's endeavors.

- **First-Acknowledge that Perfection is not Possible**
  No one is perfect. Accept this fact and feel less out of sorts. If imperfection is okay, then we're not so bad…

- **Second- Learn From your Mistakes as you Go**
  We all make them. The key is to learn so we don't make the same ones over and over. Coach Rick Pitino says that: *"Failure is just fertilizer for success."*

- **Third-Forgive Yourself and Move On**
  Don't beat yourself mentally over shortcomings. Say something like: "That's not like me," and move on. There is no sense chastising yourself for something that already happened. Self-inflicted guilt only raises feelings of inferiority.

61

- **Fourth- Offset a MIS-take with a RE-take**
  A simple little pep talk like: *"Next time, I'll know to do it this way instead of that way."* If the situation allows for it, un-do your error right then and there. On T.V. and in the movies, they call it a re-take. Well, if they can do a re-take, you can, too! Tell yourself: "Oops, take two....," then make the correction.

- **Fifth- Uplift Yourself**
  Every time you uplift yourself, you reinforce your positive self-image. You fortify your belief that you are good. You are capable of greatness. Even though you are human, you are worthy of true success.

- **Sixth- Become Your Own Best Friend**
  Discover the power of talking yourself up. Even reward yourself with a little pat on the back for a job well done. Celebrating the little victories counteracts the little slip-ups in your self-image-building efforts.

- **Seventh- Believe in You**
  Speak highly of yourself. Not in a boastful way, but in a positive, self-confident manner. Act in a confident manner. Expect good to come from all situations.

- **Eighth- Associate with those who build you up**
  You cannot afford to constantly be undermined by those whose comments or influences drag or keep you down. It becomes one step forward, two steps back. You must either correct those people, telling them you expect only uplifting comments, or get away from them. (See LESSON 401-Association).

In closing, may I suggest that you promise yourself to do what it takes to improve your self-image and increase your self-worth?

Promise Yourself

To engage in positive, uplifting
self talk at all times.

To be so strong that nothing can
disturb your peace of mind.

To talk health, happiness, and prosperity
to every person you meet.

To make your friends feel that there is
something special in each one of them.

To think only of the best, to work only
for the best and expect the very best.

To be as enthusiastic about the success
of others as you are about your own.

To forget past mistakes and focus on
greater achievements of the future.

To wear a cheerful countenance at all
times, smiling from the inside out.

To commit yourself to self-improvement,
so there's no time to criticize others.

To, above all else,
BELIEVE IN YOURSELF

Speaking and thinking highly of you

❖ How do you talk to yourself?

❖ Who is your biggest supporter? Why?

❖ Who is *not* uplifitng to you?

❖ Which of the eight steps can you use to build your self-esteem?

❖ Write an affirmation that will assist you in building a healthier self-esteem.

COMMUNICATION
Can you hear me now?

"Skill in the art of communication is crucial to a leader's success. He can accomplish nothing unless he can communicate effectively." **Norman Allen**

Are your present communication skills going to be good enough in the real world? Can your on-campus style be effective when you leave academia? Or, will you be perceived as being from another planet? I mean, *"doesn't everyone just text all the time?"* Not exactly...Let us explore these concepts and, hopefully, equip you with what you'll need to be heard in the marketplace.

Communicating effectively is a complex and challenging task. Through communication, we share our ideas, information and opinions with other people. For you to be successful in both your professional and in your personal life, you need to become an effective communicator. Through effective communication, your information or messages can be received, be understood and generate the response you desire. You can be a person of influence *only* if you become an effective communicator.

A recent Harvard study found that for every firing due to failure to perform, there were two firings due to personality conflicts and communication issues. Students study, take tests, and complete assignments predominantly in individual settings throughout their academic career.

However, the professional environment requires communication and teamwork with those of vastly different ages, cultures, and backgrounds. As the new kid on the block, you'll also have to co-exist with different personality types, such as egomaniacs, rule-breakers, brown-nosers, and the "bare-minimum-to-get-by" guy.

While your first thought might be "Well, I just won't bother with those type of people," the fact is you'll probably need to communicate with them and so many others. The goal is to get the job done, and it most often requires getting along with as many types as possible. So, play nice...

COMMUNICATION 21st CENTURY-STYLE

"The newest computer can merely compound, at speed, the oldest problem in the relations between human beings, and in the end the communicator will be confronted with the old problem, of what to say and how to say it." **Edward R. Murrow**

Text messaging -- e-mails--cell phones--instant messaging--social networks...So many ways to communicate, so many ways to MIS-communicate.

In these early years of the 21st century, the everyday options available to communicate have never been greater. Yet, if we decide to only use our preferred form of communication, it may result in mis-fires. So, how do we know when to text? When to e-mail, IM, etc? Well, the simplest way is to ask. Ask the person you are to communicate with which form or forms *they* prefer.

We are finding that there is no "one size fits all." When it comes to choosing the most appropriate form, the worst thing you can do is to guess. If what you have to say is important enough to spend time developing your information and formulating it effectively, then it is worth the time to find out which form of communication is most appropriate for this encounter.

Even more important than your choice of which channel of communication to use is what language is appropriate for the situation.

While text acronyms are fine with your peers, during informal and casual chat, they do not always translate well. Let me give you an example:

A message is received: *"btw, i wuz jw if u can m4c. can do netime, cuz nm hap'n here. cul8tr,roz."* Now, to some of you this might be as clear as day. You are ready to text back because you totally understand the message and you are anxious to meet. To others, this is just plain hieroglyphics, some foreign language that you are unable to translate. (Translation: "By the way, I was just wondering if you can meet for coffee. I can do anytime, because there's not much happening here. See you later, Roz").

Luanne Proko, business professor at Nichols College offers some advice on the matter. She suggests that you "analyze your audience for any type of communication in any chosen channel. It might be okay to use acronyms with your friends, but if you are communicating with your boss (or potential boss), who may well be a baby boomer, you need to spell it out."

Professor Proko adds: "All business e-mails should be written as though you are writing a business letter or a memo. This includes a salutation, good grammar, and an appropriate subject line."

As the President of Junior Achievement of Central Massachusetts, Deb Hopkins is constantly interacting with young adults. She is also the mother of two daughters. When it comes to the subject of the high tech communication tools and skills, Deb offers these helpful etiquette tips:

- Always avoid checking e-mails and phone messages during classes and meetings.
- Remove the Bluetooth from your ear when meeting with professional people or in professional settings.
- Text messaging while in the middle of a face-to-face conversation is rude.
- Choose the appropriate style language for the situation.

Deb shared a story about her daughter preparing an e-mail to send to her professor, and starting it with *"Would u plez."* *Deb* suggested that she address this professor as if he were standing in her presence, then use the same language in her e-mail.

As we go through a typical day, we continually adjust our communication style based on what is situation appropriate. It is vital that we make the adjustments when communicating utilizing the technology tools of today.

So, whether you are OTP (on the phone), OTT (over the top), or just OTL (out to lunch,) it is important that the message you are sending is the message being received. Even if you are AAK (asleep at the keyboard), or DWS (driving while stupid), effective communication is the goal, so choose your words wisely.

IS ANYBODY LISTENING?

We live in a fast moving, high tech world. If a volcano erupts in Italy, a soccer championship is won in Brazil or the queen hiccups in London, word of these events reaches us within minutes, sometimes seconds, of their occurring. Yet, we sit next to someone we love and are challenged to communicate effectively.

- Peter Drucker claims that all management problems stem from miscommunication.

- Experts on marriage counseling tell us that more than half of the failed marriages stem from poor communication between husband and wife.

- Many of the major problems in the world arise from one country's inability to see things from the perspective of another country--A communication breakdown of magnanimous proportions.

Communication has been defined as "A meeting of the meanings". So then, miscommunication would mean *"a missing of the meanings,"* wouldn't it? It's not what we say, but what the other person *hears* that is the starting point of the communication breakdown.

We can only increase our effectiveness in conveying our thoughts, ideas, and intentions by improving our ability to communicate. How do we do this? First, let's explore the other persons motivation for listening to us. Then, let us play *to* that motivation. What do they get from our interaction? That is really what keeps them attentive to our message.

CONNECTING WITH OTHERS

The ultimate goal of communication is to make a connection with another person or people. Most people think that if they want to be a real good communicator, they need to be a "good talker." Au contraire, mon frère. In English, just the opposite, my brother.

The number one rule for becoming an effective communicator is to become a sincere listener. Remember this, we were born with two ears and one mouth; use them in that proportion. People don't care how much you know until they know how much you care. Seek to understand before you seek to be understood.

The four core elements of communication are:

- Understanding others
- Being understood
- Being accepted
- Producing a desired response

To understand others, particularly in face-to-face encounters, we must first become active listeners. Easier said than done. It takes practice. It doesn't seem to come naturally. Most often, we are anxiously waiting for the other person to take a breath so we can get a word in. We're kind of half listening for the pause, so we can get our two cents in.

To Be an Active Listener:

- **Zone in** on what is being said. Make it important.... *really* take an interest in their message.

- **Shut off** the ever-present temptation of preparing your response.

- **Lean in** toward the person speaking. This helps you stay tuned in and your body language also tells the other person that you really are interested in them and their message.

- **Focus**... Stay with them. Retrain your eyes to stay on the speaker, not wander every time someone else walks by or speaks. It is so obvious when we do this, and we show the other person no respect. Yet, when it is our turn, we expect their undivided attention. Remember the Golden Rule: Do unto others....

- **Ask** a question related to the subject. Let them know you are with them. For example, let's say your friend is commenting about how Professor Martin seems to favor people who email with him between classes. You might interject something like: *"Now, let me see if I understand what you are saying. In your opinion, if we e-mail Professor Martin, we have a better chance of getting a higher grade in his class?"* And then stop. Let them pick it up again. They were not done. You are practicing active listening. They'll get it, especially if you allow them to now complete their thought. They will sense your interest and you will be taking communication to the next level.

- **Avoid** the mindless nod, the standard "uh-huh," or the "I hear ya" when in fact you're somewhere else mentally. Believe me, they can tell…can't you? Keep in mind that these new habits will not come easily. I have observed that by practicing them, you will put yourself far ahead of 99% of the people out there. If communication is *the* most important skill to master to improve the quality of our lives, then it is so worth it to stay committed to a constant state of improvement.

President Lyndon Johnson had a sign hanging in his office that read: *"You ain't learnin' nothin' if you're doin' all the talkin'."*

I once conveyed to a mentor that I felt that I was a good communicator, but my lifelong goal was to become a great communicator. Why is this a key goal of mine? It's very simple. I have observed that the more effective a communicator a person becomes, the stronger and healthier their self-esteem grows. Having friends, business associates and family validate them as great connectors becomes a valued reward for the effort of self-improvement. They become more comfortable in their own skin.

David Schwartz in the classic book *The Magic of Thinking Big* said: "Big people monopolize listening, small people monopolize talking." Decide to be a BIG person. Develop the skill of understanding before being understood and you earn a reputation of being a terrific conversationalist. Let's face it, most people's favorite subject is themselves. As you take an interest in them, you create a win-win proposition. First, you grow, and then, they'll appreciate you. They walk away thinking you are the greatest communicator in the world. Well, you're getting there!

Effective communication is *the* most vital skill to have a successful life--in work, in family matters, even in the spiritual sense. The better we learn to communicate, the more harmonious our life becomes. This is not the easiest thing to get good at. Yet, it is vital. It takes a lifetime commitment. It is *that* important!

John Gray wrote the best selling book *"Men are from Mars, Women are from Venus"*. Most of us guys agree with him, don't we? We sometimes are challenged, mystified even, by how what we are saying is not being received by members of the opposite sex. I know in my marriage, this is a constant challenge. Yet, I am committed to my relationship with Linda. I want the best for her and our family. Therefore, I needed to grow in my ability to communicate in spite of the fact that we are from different planets. As a matter of fact, I needed to deny the planetary differences so that we could communicate effectively. It was not an option. It was a must do.

You will find the same to be true. If the person, or people, you want to communicate with are important to you, then your decision is a no-brainer. It becomes "we must communicate here, so let's figure out how".

"What air is to the body, to be understood is to the heart."
~Steven Covey~

COMMUNICATION 101

Here are some very basic steps you can take to become a most effective communicator:

<u>When You are Speaking:</u>

- **Smile.** It will put the other person in a better frame of mind to receive your message.

- **Prepare your thoughts**, so your message is clear.

- **Call them by name.** The sweetest sound to another's ears is the sound of their own name.

- **Make eye contact.** Look at people when you speak. No need to stare, but look into their face every 10-15 seconds.

- **Speak with clarity,** Loud enough and clearly. Watch your body language, you want to be friendly and confident in your message and open to discussion.

- **Take a breath**. Do not run on and on. Give others a chance to respond…and confirm you are going in the right direction.

- **Vary your pitch and inflection.** Monotones are out.

- **Exude enthusiasm**. Enthusiasm is important, yet don't be overbearing like you're trying to "sell" them something.

- **Show respect.** Thank them. Appreciate their time and their opinions on the subject discussed.

When Others Speak:

- **Clear your head.** Give them your mental attention.

- **Acknowledge what they are saying.** Convey interest by a nod, or a response showing you're "getting it."

- **Repeat part of their message.** "So, what you are saying is…"

- **Ask questions.** "So, which section would go first?"

- **Stay alert.** No yawning, or reading something while they speak, and no texting either.

- **Make eye contact.** Again, lock in, but don't stare.

- **Don't jump to conclusions**. Hear them out. You are both in a position to learn something.

- **Respect differing viewpoints.** Ours is not the only solution. Others bring a perspective we just don't see.

- **One-upping is not good.** Possibly the most annoying exercise of all. Don't play "I can do you one better". It will not win you any points.

- **Facial expressions.** Try not to show displeasure as they speak. Hear their ideas out first. Showing displeasure during their message tends to shut down both parties.

Practice these…make them yours. Review them from time to time. These are not optional if you desire to become an effective communicator. They are essential.

THE INDIAN TALKING STICK

"When people talk, listen completely.
Most people never listen."
~Ernest Hemingway~

There is an ancient ritual practiced among Indian tribes that can serves as an excellent tool for effective communication. It is reverently referred to as the Talking Stick. Here's how it works:

When two or more people come together to discuss an important matter, one will bring the Talking Stick to the meeting. The first person to speak holds the stick. Everyone else listens without interruption until the person holding the stick speaks their mind.

When they have completed their thoughts, then, and only then, do they pass the stick to the next person who has their opportunity to express themselves. The conversation continues, as the stick is passed along.

The key is to listen to each other…hear each other out, rather than mentally defending your own beliefs. The physical presence of the stick forces each person to focus on the one speaking. Their point of view is important. While they hold the stick, they are the one and only source of input at that time. You, knowing that your time to hold the stick will come, must contain your opinions until they are through.

The message here, and it is a most important one in communicating, is to "seek to understand before we seek to be understood." If, in all of our interactions with others, we totally embrace this philosophy, there would be a lot less miscommunication. When there is more effective communication, there is more peace in the valley. Thus, *our* world, and *the* world will be a better place to work and live.

PUT YOUR HEART INTO IT

"The words are not nearly as important as the music"
Uncle Dave

It's not how much you know, it's how much you can communicate. It's not what you say, it's what they hear. Put another way, it is not what I *think* I said, it is what they believe they heard. Stop thinking about what makes sense to you. Start thinking about what makes sense to them.

So often, the message that leaves our mouths are not the same as the one that reaches the other person. As you learn to communicate heart to heart whenever possible, you can then by-pass the brain with all of its filters and prejudgmental ways.

If you care...if the other person really matters to you, then it is of the utmost importance that you connect...not just talk *at* each other, but connect ...spiritually, if you will, heart to heart...soul to soul. If you are playing a tune of "I care," instead of "I hear," then your level of effective communication rises immensely. Further, if your actions are consistent with your words, you are on a communication level that can seldom be reached by mere words alone.

So, be sincere...care. Mean what you say. Listen to me... hear me... connect with me... When I know that what I am saying is important to you, then I know that *I am important to you.*

When I believe this, I can trust you and your words have meaning. In this world, where integrity is so often compromised and words don't seem to mean a thing, as you display personal integrity in your interpersonal relationships, you stand above the crowd.

You will be a person whom others with integrity will want to be with. So, say what you mean and mean what you say. I can trust that. The world wants that!

Effective, integrity-based communication begins and ends with *sincerity*--With it, we grow--Without it, we go.

"If you establish common ground with the other person, they will like you, believe you, begin to trust you, connect with you on a deeper level---A "things-in-common" level. The best way to win connection is to first win the person."
~Jeffrey Gitomer~

Communication Self-Assessment:

❖ How well do you connect with others in your peer group? Explain.

_____

❖ How well do you connect with others older than you? Explain.

_____

❖ Do you consider yourself a good listener?

_____

❖ Which of the communication skills discussed do you feel are your strengths?

_____

❖ Which of the communication areas discussed do you need to improve?

_____

OBSTACLES
Get Over Them and Win

"Stand up to your obstacles and do something about them. You'll find that they haven't half the strength you think they have." **Norman Vincent Peale**

WHAT I LEARNED FROM THE CIRCUS

"How is it that you can stake down a ten-ton elephant with the same size stake that you use for a little baby one?" I asked. "It's easy if you know two things: Elephants do have great memories, but they aren't very smart. When they are babies, we stake them down. They try to tug away from the stake maybe ten thousand times before they realize that they can't possibly get away. At that point, their elephant memory takes over and they remember for the rest of their lives that they can not get away from the stake." So no matter how big he gets, he cannot enjoy freedom because he thinks he can't.

That was me: shackled by my past, unable to see that I was no longer a little boy sitting on the curb in the project waiting for my step-dad to come and take us somewhere exciting (he "forgot to come"). I was much bigger than that now. I could make my own choices, if only I knew I could. Yet, just like that elephant, for so long I wouldn't even try because I knew I couldn't break free.

How about you? Is there a small stake and a shackle holding you back from reaching for your dreams? If so, it's time to grab some inner strength and give that shackle a yank. Flush out the limiting past beliefs and begin to live up to your full potential. Do that, and believe me, the world will look (and smell) a whole lot better than a three-ring circus.

FAILURE BEFORE SUCCESS

English novelist John Creasey got 753 rejection slips before he published 564 books. Babe Ruth struck out 1,330 times, but he also hit 714 home runs. Don't worry about failures. Worry about chances you miss when you don't even try. George Lucas, the filmmaker of *Star Wars* fame, said:

"You have to find something that you love enough to be able to take risks, jump over the hurdles, and break through the brick walls that are always going to be placed in front of you. If you don't have that kind of feeling for what it is you're doing, you'll stop at the first giant hurdle."

Many consider Ted Williams the greatest hitter of all time. Modern day baseball players use his principles to become the best. Yet, in his finest year, the champion failed at the plate about sixty percent of the time.

Football's greatest quarterbacks complete only six out of ten passes. The best basketball players make only one half their shots. Even with the use of all the 21st century technology like satellite mapping and expert geologists, oil companies make strikes in only one out of ten wells.

Actors, auditioning for roles are turned down twenty-nine of thirty times. And stock market winners make money on only two out of five of their investments.

Michael Jordan on failing his way to success:

"I missed more than 9,000 shots in my career. I lost almost 300 games. On 26 occasions, I was entrusted to take the game winning shot...and missed. I have failed over and over and over again in my life. That is precisely why I succeed."

THE UNDERDOG

WHO AM I?---My freshman high school team was 0-8. I was the seventh string quarterback in college. I was drafted in the sixth round...the 199th pick. When I made the pros, I was the fourth string quarterback. So far, you might think that this person *never* made it. A seventh stringer ...199th pick? They just aren't good enough...usually.

Now, add: Sportsman of the Year, three Super Bowl wins, Most Valuable Player and the name Tom Brady is the only answer. Tom offers advice to those who are not yet superstars: "Be prepared for your opportunity, so when it does come, you make the most of it."

How did Brady prepare for that opportunity? By working longer and harder than most were willing to work. He used the "underdog" mentality as his driving force to succeed. Tom claims that he is not naturally gifted. He knew that sixth-rounders are not supposed to make it in the NFL. But that didn't defeat him---it motivated him.

It was his insecurity that drove him to prepare longer and harder than the rest. He believed that someday he would get his chance to prove himself and he constantly worked so that he would be ready to make the most of that opportunity. And that he did. Brady's favorite quote: "The only place success comes before work is in the dictionary."

Successful people agree that you've got to put in hard work and be prepared to reach the top. *It will be worth it!*

TOXIC WASTE

Now there's a subject that's often in the news. The toxins addressed here, however, are not the ones that pollute the planet. They are those that we often allow to pollute our thinking. Toxic behaviors like whining, procrastination, and the victim mentality (a.k.a "The poor me syndrome"). Others can be more serious such as substance abuse, dishonesty, physical or psychological abuse, negative emotions like hatred, jealousy, anger, and resentment.

Each of us has some toxic waste that holds us back from greater success, and blocks the blessings of life like joy, love and prosperity. It slows us down, drains positive energy, keeping us from reaching our full potential.

To move forward in a positive direction, we must remove ourselves from constant contact with toxic people. We need to find ways to eliminate toxic forces in our habits, in our attitudes, and in our environment.

You *do* have control over the decision to change and eliminate many of these elements. Decide to change those that you can and seek help for those that require professional help. Your future depends on it.

THE GREATEST SALESMAN IN THE WORLD

"A natural salesman. Born with the gift. Could sell snowballs to Eskimos." These are phrases often repeated when referring to successful salespeople. Og Mandino wrote a classic book called *The Greatest Salesman in The World.* A pretty bold statement, if he was writing about himself. Well, the true story about Og's life is far from the title of his classic book.

After an honorable military career as a bomber pilot in World War II, Og Mandino found it difficult to get a job. So, he became an insurance salesman. Traveling on the road, sitting in bars, Mandino became an alcoholic. He was unable to keep a job. His wife left him and took their only child. Mandino overcame his toxic behavior, replaced it with an enormous appetite for reading and went on to write nineteen books selling *over fifty million copies.*

Here's Mandino's take on obstacles: "Obstacles are necessary for success. As in all careers, victory comes only after many struggles and countless defeats. Each struggle, each defeat, sharpens your skills and strengths, your courage and endurance, ability and confidence, thus each obstacle is a comrade-in-arms forcing you to become better... or quit. Each rebuff is an opportunity to move forward; turn away from them, avoid them, and you throw away your future."

Plain and simple language... You either decide to use the obstacle to move forward, *or* throw away your future. Just the way I like it. No minced words...just the facts.

WHAT'S EATING YOU?

Got something that's bothering you? Write out in a clear, complete statement, the challenge you are facing. Ask yourself, "What are the causes of this situation?" Spend some quality, uninterrupted time, allowing yourself to clearly state the matter. Often you resolve it right there. If not, then ask yourself, "What are all the possible answers to this challenge?" Write them out---brainstorm, don't evaluate. Review all the answers, decide on the best possible solution, then ACT...Don't wait...do it now!

Get rid of the "Someday I'm gonna..." and the "If only..." syndromes, and get on with life! This may be a difficult thing to hear but the only person being hurt carrying this emotional baggage around is you!

LET IT GO AND YOU WILL GROW

Harboring un-forgiveness, resentment and anger is like taking poison and expecting the other person to die.

A study performed at the Harvard School of Public Health reported that those scoring highest on an anger scale were three times more likely to develop heart disease than those scoring lowest. Each day you hold on to that emotional pain and resentment, you give the person who wronged you control over your life. Each and every day drains away more and more of your own personal power.

The fact is that if we are the ones taking or holding in this toxic emotion, we are killing ourselves. They usually don't have a clue. When we forgive, we win! Forgiveness is having the courage to let go of the negative emotions you have about the person who hurt you. Researchers on forgiveness believe you are in control of your behavior and have the ability to make a personal choice to forgive or not.

Choosing to forgive is you having personal control over your own life -- instead of giving that control over to the person who hurt you. This does not mean the offending person is unaccountable for their actions. The goal of forgiveness is to take you from the place of victim to a place of improved health and greater personal power.

You're probably saying to yourself, "Yes, I'd love to let go of the heavy load I carry around, but forgiving is easier said than done." You're absolutely right. It is probably one of the most difficult things to practice.

You start the process by acknowledging your anger, fear, resentment, and grief. Your feelings are justified and should not be minimized. Understand that forgiveness does not condone the behavior that has brought you pain nor does it allow you to be abused.

It makes you the bigger person for releasing and letting go bringing immediate benefits to you and leads you on the path toward physical and emotional strength and well-being. Forgiveness is for you -- for your health, wellness, and quality of life. *Let the healing begin within.*

I never viewed myself as particularly talented.
I've viewed myself as slightly above average in talent.
Where I excel is with a ridiculous, sickening work ethic.
While other guys are sleeping, I'm working.
While the other guy's eating, I'm working."
~Will Smith~

BUSINESS SUCCESS AT 16!

When he was only 16 years old, Michael Simmons co-founded his first business, a web development company. He went on to the Stern School of Business at New York University, and founded The Extreme Entrepreneurship Education Corporation.

Here is his reply when asked what challenges he faced in building a successful business at such a young age: "The largest obstacles I've faced have been people closest to me trying to persuade me away from my passion and purpose. These obstacles are hard because they change us without us even knowing it. All the obstacles I've faced have been defeatable with optimism, persistance, and creativity."

Successful people regardless of age, overcome the obstacles around them with positive action. Michael used his journal, his focus and an unrelenting optimism to win. You will need to equip yourself with such tools to defeat whatever obstacles are in your path to success.

BORN TO SUCCEED?

What do these men have in common?

Richard Nixon--Gerald Ford--Jimmy Carter --Ronald Reagan--Bill Clinton

They were all President of The United States, right? That's the most obvious connection. Let's look a little deeper at each of their backgrounds:

Richard Nixon: Born in the home his father built, won an award from Harvard his senior year of high school. However, his family was unable to afford his leaving home for college. He instead attended Whittier College locally.

Gerald Ford: Born Leslie Lynch King, Jr. In 1913, his mother left her abusive husband and took her son to live with her parents. She met Gerald R. Ford, whom she married and gave her child his name Gerald Rudolph Ford, Jr. The only President to be adopted, Ford worked in his stepfather's paint store and coached boxing during college to afford his tuition.

Jimmy Carter: He was the first member of his family to go to college. His father was a peanut farmer.

Ronald Reagan: Son of an alcoholic traveling shoe salesman, he worked his way into show business by broadcasting baseball games. At forty, he was divorced and his career was at a dead end.

Bill Clinton: Born William Jefferson Blythe IV. His father, a traveling salesmen, died in an automobile accident three months before Bill was born. His mother married Roger Clinton and Bill took that name. His stepfather was a gambling alcoholic who regularly abused his wife, and sometimes Clinton's half brother Roger.

None of these men were born into wealth. Each of their family circumstances could have been used as their excuse for mediocrity. Most people would have let them off the hook because of their environment growing up.

Not one of them bought the excuse. They each went on to achieve the rank of most powerful person in the free world by working hard and not accepting excuses.

HANDICAP? WHAT HANDICAP?

The story of Kyle Maynard is truly a remarkable one. It is about a young man who confronted his limitations head on and loves to win. Kyle Maynard was born March 24, 1986 with a rare disorder called, "congenital amputation," leaving him with three joints: a neck and two shoulders. He has no elbows or knees. He measures just over 3 feet tall and weighs approximately 120 pounds.

Despite his physical differences, Kyle was one of the top high school wrestlers in Georgia. He competed in the 2004 Georgia High School Wrestling Championship, narrow missing All-American status.

He participates in many sports, including baseball, swimming, street hockey, football, and wrestling, without the aide of prosthetics. As impressive as his academic and sport accomplishments are, it's Kyle's attitude towards life that makes him a truly unique person. Kyle does not think in terms of limitations, only accomplishments.

One of Kyle's favorite sayings is, *"It's not what I can do; it's what I will do."* The attitude Kyle approaches life with is the result of numerous failures, the perseverance to overcome limitations, and the loving, strict care of his parents. Want some more examples? Read on...

"Life is what happens to you while you are making other plans."
~Uncle Dave~

GREAT ROLE MODELS OF PERSEVERENCE

Despite various handicaps and disabilities, these men and women went on to provide the world with great talent and discovery. Had they not chosen to be over-comers, we would not be able to celebrate their success.

Albert Einstein (scientist) - had a learning disability
Beethoven (composer) - was deaf
Franklin D. Roosevelt (President)-was paralyzed from polio
Helen Keller (author) - was deaf and blind
Itzhak Perlman (concert violinist)-waist down paralysis
James Earl Jones (actor) - was a stutterer
Marlee Matlin (actress) - is deaf
Ray Charles (musician) - was blind
Stephen Hawking (physicist) - had Lou Gehrig's disease
Stevie Wonder (musician) - is blind
Kyle Maynard (athlete) - congenital amputee
Thomas Edison (inventor) - had a learning problem
Vincent Van Gogh (artist) - was mentally ill
Woodrow Wilson (President) - had a learning disability

Did you know that Sam Walton went broke twice, Einstein was divorced, Abraham Lincoln battled depression, or that Ronald Reagan had his heart broken by his first wife? Did it make me feel better because they had hard times? Yes and no. I don't find pleasure in the misfortunes of others. It is without question that Einstein, Lincoln, Reagan and Walton were monumental successes. Yet, it is refreshing and inspiring to read that they were also human and have walked down the same road that you and I have, overcoming obstacles, and negative along their journey. I have found that negative thoughts, and feelings, stay with you only as long as you give them your attention.

If you believe you are handicapped, or disadvantaged you buy into your own negative stuff. Stop giving attention to that, and focus on your journey to revealing your great talent. The world awaits, ready to receive and applaud you.

Sheila Crump Johnson, co-founder of the BET Network, is a billionaire success story. While speaking at the commencement of Cambridge College, Ms Johnson cautioned graduates that while many will tell you to set goals for your entire life, her message was to *"prepare yourself for what opportunities life presents."* She explained, *"You have to achieve failure before you can achieve success."*

As Founder and President of Honda Motors, Soichiro Honda knew a thing or two about overcoming failure on the way to success. He said "Many people dream of success. To me success can be achieved only through repeated failure and introspection. Success only represents one percent of your work that results from 90 percent of failure. Very few unacquainted with failure ever know the true joy of success."

George Washington Carver put it this way: "Ninety-nine percent of failures come from people who have the habit of making excuses."

I will always remember Les Brown's three steps to take during "hard times":

1. **Have Faith** (The apostle Paul said, "Faith is the substance of things hoped for...")
2. **Remind yourself:** "No matter how hard it is or how hard it gets, I'm going to make it!"
3. **Have patience** and engage in consistent action.

So, whatever your obstacle, do us all a big favor... GET OVER IT! Life is too short to make excuses. Set your goals and pursue them. If you have been dealt a 'worse' hand than another, it may indeed be a gift that teaches you the value of hard work. Your story will be richer and your success even sweeter when you achieve your dreams.

Who knows, maybe one day I will cast a vote for *YOU as President of The United States!*

Cool ways to cope with obstacles:

- *Be under control as you express your feelings.*
- *Face and accept what happens in your life.*
- *Find and use positive quotes from someone who persisted and won.*
- *Gain knowledge from others' experiences.*
- *Get help if you need it.*
- *Go see a good movie about an overcomer, ...like Rocky, Sea Biscuit or Rudy.*
- *Learn and grow from your experiences, including the ones that hurt.*
- *Seek a role model for inspiration to persist.*
- *Take a break. Chill...*
- *Work it out.*
- *Write about your feelings. Get it out.--Journal it.*

Not-so-cool ways to cope with obstacles
Don't:

- Blame yourself
- Blame other people
- Blame chance
- Blame other things, forces, or powers
- Escape or avoid your problems
- Lose your cool
- Quit

"Success is to be measured not so much by the position that one has reached in life as by the obstacles which one has overcome while trying to succeed." **Booker T. Washington**

Obstacles—Get over them

❖ Can you identify one or two obstacles that are
   holding you back from greatness?

❖ What do you do to cope with challenges in life?

❖ Do you have a successful role model?

❖ Do you need to remove any toxins from your life?

❖ Who do you know who is an overcomer?   Why?

DON'T QUIT

When things go wrong as they sometimes will,
When the road you're trudging seems all uphill.
When the funds are low and the debts are high,
And you want to smile but you have to sigh.

When care is pressing you down a bit,
Rest if you must, but don't you quit.
Life is queer with its twists and turns,
As everyone of us sometimes learns.

And many a fellow turns about,
When he might have won had he stuck it out.
Don't give up though the pace seems slow,
You may succeed with another blow.

Often the goal is nearer than
It seems to a faint and faltering man.
Often the struggler has given up,
When he might have captured the victor's cup.

And he learned too late when the night came down,
how close he was to the golden crown.
Success is failure turned inside out,
The silver tint of the clouds of doubt.

And you never can tell how close you are,
It may be near when it seems afar.
So stick to the fight when you're hardest hit,
It's when things seem worst that you mustn't quit.

BRANDING YOURSELF
Be Like Tiger, Jeff Gordon, Rachel Ray

Education is wonderful. Landing a good job is just the beginning. Do you want to know the truth? Here it is: From here on out, it's not about the education you got, or which school you graduate from. It's not all about the job. It's all about Y-O-U...I call it YOU, INC. *Your* career ...*Your* image...*Your* branding.

Life is a series of new beginnings. Just as finishing school is one beginning, so, too, is getting that first job. It is the beginning of your creating a "best-selling" career. And one of the best strategies for creating such a life is to create a brand that has enduring qualities, one that is built to last. When you build your brand on traits that you can be proud of, you are building for the long road. Built to last a lifetime, not just for a season.

BY DESIGN, NOT LUCK

Decide to build your career by design, not by luck. Leaving it to chance is no better than employing a "buy a lottery ticket" approach to success. I have found that those who just let life determine how things happen are often disappointed with the results. As the years roll on, they often look in the mirror and ask "What happened? Where did the time go? Where did my life go?"

Choose, instead to build your personal brand on goals and dreams and a quest for success. Strive for excellence. By doing so, you improve the controllable factors to 80%, while reducing "luck" to a mere 20%. The odds for success are more favorable when you decide on the proper brand, then commit to growing that brand.

STARPOWER

Jeff Gordon was fourteen when he walked into Valvoline's office attempting to get free oil for his sprint car. When asked how he'd gotten there, the kid replied without so much as a grin, *"My mom drove me. How about that oil?"* Ever since, he and his team have been building a portfolio that includes two dozen companies, including DuPont, Pepsi, GMAC and Nicorette.

So, how did they develop such a powerful brand? John Bickford, his business manager and stepfather sorts it all out. "It's all geared toward brand strategy. Just like Tiger Woods, our brand is a name, a personality. So we constantly ask, how would this really reflect on Jeff?" It's a constant consciousness of how every association, every appearance, every statement affects the brand that they have carefully crafted Jeff Gordon—the brand."

So it is with us. We, too, must be diligent in our associations. We need to weigh what we say and how we look in order to grow our personal brand. *Our* brand should be the most important brand to us. After all, it is the *only* one we've got. If we think on these terms, we are placing more value on the things that can make us a *BIG* success in life including our chosen profession. Otherwise, we are likely to be stuck in the middle of the pack with a weak, forgettable brand. Choose wisely. It *will* make a difference.

PLAY IT FORWARD

It was a beautiful morning in March. We were traveling to a five star resort in Florida for a little R&R-- A nice place to spend some time away from a New England winter. With six more hours to go, I had driven far enough for one day and decided to spend the night at an Inn just off the Interstate. After a nights rest, I made my way over to get some coffee and the morning paper. As I passed by, I saw someone removing those huge trash bags from the covered barrels.---Travelers have a habit of leaving stuff behind to lighten their load. The fella emptying it caught my eye. He looked familiar. As I returned with our morning "caffeine fix" and paper, I got another glimpse and, yes, I *did* know this guy.

"Dan Murray?" I inquired. Yes, it was! We had graduated from school together. He was the good looking, popular "A" student. I was the guy who had to go to work right after school to afford it. He was voted "Most likely to succeed." I was not voted anything."

We chatted briefly and I asked him how he had "landed" here. He explained his journey and summarized by explaining that, at some point, he had chosen *not* to continue pursuing career advancement. Instead, choosing to "check out and find myself." Well, we exchanged best wishes and I went on my way.

As we pulled out to complete our journey to oceanfront luxury, my mind would not let go of this chance encounter. Hundreds of miles from where we both grew up, I got to reflect on what might have been.

Here, I was, the guy with the decent grades and limited popularity heading to a five star resort. And, there was Dan, Mr. Popularity with the brains, emptying another trash can still trying to "find himself."

What's the lesson here, you ask. It seemed to me that Dan had a very good brand while we were in school. It wasn't, however, one that he actually had anything to do with creating. He was born with the good looks. He seemed gifted with smarts and grew up in a good neighborhood.

Yet, when he hit the real world and had to make decisions, he decided to take the easy road and check out, rather than pay the price to gain a more meaningful life. His choice defined his brand.

MORAL: It's not the brand you start out with that matters, but the brand you choose to build for yourself. Don't let what you had no control of determine your fate. If you don't make choices, life has a way of doing it for you. And you might not like where you end up.

Advice from Uncle Dave: *Choose to build a brand on quality. Choose to make tough decisions that will serve you well for the long haul. Choose to grow in your career and find yourself along the way...*
> ...Choose the Resort over the Trash.

RESUMÉ IS THE FIRST PIECE OF YOUR BRAND

Leaders work at becoming their own brand. Your resumé is the first step in branding yourself. Your grades are an indication of how well you did in a certain subject. They are just one piece of the picture. Then, there are the extra-curricular activities, the clubs you joined, the community service you performed and so forth.

All of these components fit together to give your potential employer a snapshot of who you are *today*. Your intangible attributes are not always evident on a piece of paper. These you must bring to the career day, the interviews, and ultimately, the workplace. There are still many opportunities for you to show your true colors. And, believe me, they want to see them.

They all want to know what you stand for. Are you trustworthy? A team player? An effective communicator? Do you stand for integrity? Is it below you to provide great service? Will you develop a reputation as a hard worker, 110% satisfaction guaranteed? Or one who offers up a weak, part time effort?

Is your attitude "Whatever," or "Whatever it takes?" Each one of these attributes makes you either an asset or liability. Companies are *not* looking to take on more liability, for sure. Choose to be an asset and you can climb higher than you have yet to imagine.

If, after you do a little self-analysis, you decide your brand needs an overhaul, then the first step is to develop some new habits. Stick to them. If, for example, your attitude is lacking, then clean it up...Check your self-talk. *What is going on up there?*

Here's the best way for you to test it out. Ask yourself "Which brand would I buy?" Do you prefer the one you can trust or the "whatever?" Is your preference to get good service or one with "attitude"...the *wrong* kind.

I know in the workplace, a winning brand has the right qualities. If you want to be that winner, then brand yourself with the right stuff...and win, baby.

Is your communication clear, professional and conducive to the workplace you are looking to enter? If not, what habit must you form? Go right down the list.

Ask someone who is in the workplace for an honest assessment. "What do I need to change to be an asset to the workplace I wish to be in?" This is not an easy thing to do. But, neither is wallowing in mediocrity and wondering why you're not getting ahead. If facing up to reality *now* saves you a lot of disappointment later, then it is worth it.

WHICH WOLF ARE YOU FEEDING?

Habits define your brand. Repetition forms a habit.

A grandfather was walking along with his little grandson. And the little boy asked, "Grandpa, how come some people are nice and happy and others are sad?"

The grandpa explained "Son, there are two wolves fighting inside each of us. One wolf is full of fear, hatred, greed, lies and selfishness. The other is full of faith, joy, peace, kindness and love."

After some thought and a few more steps, the little boy inquired "Grandpa, which wolf is going to win inside me?" "Son," grandpa replied, "it's the one you feed that will win inside of you."

Feeding the "wolf" is a habit. The actions you choose to repeat will create your brand. So, remember, YOU are your brand for success. Choose wisely.

BRAND PERCEPTION

"See yourself as your own brand: Think SUCCESS."
~ Uncle Dave~

Identifying your brand begins with how you are perceived. If you cheapen the brand early, it's tougher to go for quality later.

Samsung exemplifies the importance of brand perception. The giant Korean electronics manufacturer was known as a purveyor of cheap knockoffs back in the 80's and 90's. In an attempt to change their image and re-brand themselves, Samsung began emphasizing research and development, quality management and technological innovation. However, many years and hundreds of millions of dollars later, the company still struggles to get the respect they are earning.

It's not too early to decide what *YOU*, the brand will stand for. In fact, if you commit to quality, integrity, a willingness to learn and other positive attributes, *you will not have to explain your past reputation!*

BUILD THE *YOU* BRAND

Here are some branding ideas that have worked for other students:

Business Cards: Have some made up with your name, contact information, etc. Under your name, put student, perhaps with your major, or area of interest. Like "Future Engineer or Aspiring T.V. Producer." Use a creative way to express your intent when you graduate.

While working on the production crew of our *Success Journey* television program, my son Josh heard a guest suggest that students have a business card. Josh was a college sophomore and like many students didn't have a clear path as to what he want to do with his life. It all changes in a New York minute. So, he simply chose "Difference Maker" as a title...for now. That much, Josh was sure of... He knew he wanted to make a difference.

Create Sound Bites: Develop a short description of your career goal, so you can answer the question: *"What do you want to do when you get out of school?"* in a clear, yet concise way. Some people call this an elevator speech. Imagine you are in the elevator going to the top...of course. As someone gets on, you exchange pleasantries. They are taken by your presence, your pleasant upbeat attitude, your smile and your style. Then they ask you the magic question *"What are you going to do when you graduate?" Or, "What do you do?"* Just as begin to answer you realize they are getting off at the next stop... Are you ready to give them an answer and STILL have time to give them your card before they step off?

That, my friends, is an elevator speech. What are you going to say? Prepare one and then memorize it. Who knows, you just might be speaking with the person who can open the door to your big career break.

Create a video: A CD, a DVD, or streaming video makes you stand out in this 21st Century E-world we all live in. A video resume' is becoming more and more popular. Go to: www.careertv.com See if this is a fit for you.

Get a Mentor: Someone to model your brand after. Look for a person you respect who has qualities you'd like to develop. Ask them if you could buy them coffee now and then to learn from them. It's important you respect and value their time. They probably have responsibilities that restrict their time and availability.

Create a Personal Website: Beyond MySpace or Facebook ...Check out Squidoo and Flickr or Linkedin. Create a personal site where you can put your best foot forward. You might direct potential employers to these sites or burn it to a CD... Call it your electronic business card and provide it at your interviews.

Be careful what you put up on Facebook or other social sites. While your friends may admire your photo at a keg party, potential employees won't see it that way. According to John McGrath, Director of Career Services at Providence College, "Ethical norms matter in certain industries and *really* matter in others. They certainly *don't* want young people who are indiscreet." McGrath advises: *"As you near the job search, clean up your Facebook."*

THE LOOK OF SUCCESS

"Don't let your clothes, your image, your manners or your overall 'look' sabotage your chances for success. Put your best foot forward everyday and take on the persona of your brand." **Uncle Dave**

If you feel and act like you belong, then you will "fit" better in your career environment. The way you dress is a key part of your "brand." Don't take it lightly. No one enjoys being judged for a job based on looks. We'd rather be hired because of our skills and abilities.

But like it or not, appearance matters in the interview and on the job. Your appearance sends a message to potential employers about your motivation, professionalism, and overall "fit" within the organization.

It's a reality -- people who look good make more money, get promoted faster and often most likely to enjoy lifelong success. A Clairol study reported that women who wear properly applied make-up enjoy higher salaries. So, look your best to improve your odds for advancement.

THREE SIMPLE RULES FOR BUSINESS DRESS

"Clothes make the man. Naked people have little or no influence on society." **Mark Twain**

There are three main categories of business dress: Business, business casual, and casual. While there are no absolute rules regarding dress, here are some guidelines: When interviewing on-campus, always opt for business dress. Likewise, if you interview off-campus assume that business dress is called for, unless you research and find out otherwise. West Coast interview attire is less formal.

The primary goal of dressing for your interview is to feel good and look professional. If you feel uncomfortable in an outfit, even if people say you look great, don't wear it. Have someone help you select an outfit that looks professional and feels great.

When in doubt, always overdress and be more conservative than you normally might.

THINGS TO AVOID:
- Rumpled clothes
- Scuffed shoes
- Ratty nails
- Wild sport/t-shirts
- Athletic clothing
- Sneakers
- Hiking boots
- Flip flops

WOMEN

Avoid:

- Short shorts
- Camisoles
- Mini-skirts
- Low-cut tops
- Bright nails
- Strong fragrances
- Excessive make-up

Wear dark colors. They make you look slimmer, more fit, influential and more confident. A jacket or a blazer always makes you appear more in control.

DEVELOPING YOUR BEST BRAND

"Just make up your mind at the very outset that your work is going to stand for quality, that you are going to stamp a superior quality upon everything that goes out of your hands, that whatever you do shall bear the hallmark of excellence." **Orison Sweet Marden**

Branding yourself, in personal and professional life, is most valuable. You achieve social confidence and a balanced life by setting effective boundaries. It's vital to be true to your brand and diligent in protecting and improving upon it. Buy into these values and you'll be branded a *winner*-A person whom I would like to associate with, do business with and be proud to call a friend.

TOP TEN TIPS FOR A WINNING BRAND

- **BE RELIABLE**. Be a person who can be counted on. Train yourself to be *"early* on time."

- **BE TRUSTWORTHY**. Say what you mean and mean what you say.

- **BE RESPECTFUL**. From the boss to the cleaning crew, we are all humans looking to be appreciated. Say hello. Thank you. Please.
     R-E-S-P-E-C-T. If you want it, give it.

- **BE HAPPY**. Smile, be friendly, have a cheerful outlook.

- **BE POSITIVE**. See the glass as half-full. Be upbeat and optimistic in your outlook.

- **BE TEACHABLE**. Always seek the opportunity to learn. It's the key to advancement.

- **BE A TEAM PLAYER**. There is no "I" in team. "Many hands make for light work."

- **BE A PERSON OF INTEGRITY**. Do the right thing. Don't compromise your values. Associate your brand with others who live with integrity.

- **BE ENTHUSIASTIC**. Enthusiasm matters. It's contagious. Take on tough assignments-stay late-come in early-whatever it takes to get the job done. If you're not enthusiastic about what you do, do something else.

- **BE PROUD**. Pour your best into your work, so you will gladly put your name on the finished product. Be proud of what you stand for, and settle for nothing less than EXCELLENCE.

The Man In The Glass

When you get what you want in your struggle for self
And the world makes you king for a day,
Just go to the mirror and look at yourself
And see what that man has to say.

For it isn't your father or mother or wife
Whose judgment upon you must pass.
The fellow whose verdict counts most in you life
Is the one staring back from the glass.

You may be like Jack Horner and chisel a plum
And think you're a wonderful guy.
But the man in the glass says you're only a bum
If you can't look him straight in the eye.

He's the fellow to please-never mind all the rest,
For he's with you clear to the end.
And you've passed your most dangerous, difficult test
If the man in the glass is your friend.

You may fool all the world down the pathway of years
And get pats on the back as you pass.
But your final reward will be heartache and tears
If you've cheated the man in the glass.

ARE YOU BRANDED?

❖   Define the qualities of your present brand.

_____

❖   Who do you emulate as a brand? Why?

_____

❖   What brand will you develop in the next ten years?

_____

❖   What action will you take to improve your brand?

_____

❖   What will your "Ultimate" brand be like?

_____

"A leader is one who knows the way, goes the way, and shows the way."

~John Maxwell~

21st CENTURY LEADERSHIP
Lead, Follow, or Get Out of the Way

"The supreme quality for leadership is unquestionably integrity. Without it, no real success is possible."
~Dwight D. Eisenhower~

Here is a good question to ask yourself: Ten years from now you will surely arrive. The question is, where? Looking back, I am certain that how you embrace leadership will have a huge impact on where you arrive. And that begins with leadership in your personal life first.

Leadership is a living organism, growing and changing all the time and you're contributing to that growth. I don't believe that people set out to be leaders. They set out to be managers, engineers, accountants, sales people, moms, dads, researchers, rabbis, ministers, politicians, firemen, actors, etc.

With a commitment to personal and professional development, we take hold of our future and position ourselves for leadership in the most important aspects of life. Be it with our spouses, children or co-workers, our ability to lead is limited only by our own expansion.

Every obstacle that you face is an opportunity to learn and grow. The more impossible a challenge seems, the more you stand to benefit as you rise to the occasion and whip that challenge. Thus, the more prepared you are when you are called upon to lead.

I did not have the luxury of growing up in an environment that offered any role models of strong, effective leaders. As a project kid, my self-image did not allow me to believe that I could someday own a multi-million dollar company and lead and train others around the world. For me to get into such positions, I had to grow; expand my capacities. My leadership skills began with *me* leading me, developing the right habits and then being open to the process of being a protégé, mentored by those who were much wiser than I.

MENTORS

> *"It is other people's experience that makes the older man wiser than the younger man."* **Yoruba Proverb**

I've been most fortunate to be mentored, directly and indirectly, by some incredibly wise people. It is because of my great fortune that I am able to share some of this wisdom with you. Yet, when it comes to mentors and mentoring, you should manage your expectations. If you set out to find an incredibly wise guru who can offer you endless amounts of time and extoll unlimited amounts of life-changing advice, you will be disappointed.

Never once did I have the most successful person in my field sit down for large amounts of time and give me their undivided attention. In reality, it's a nugget of wisdom here, a shared experience there. I'll pick up a success tip from a book, learn a valuable lesson at a conference or from an audio recording. I am constantly being mentored.

ANTHONY "SPAG" BORGATTI

I recall getting simple, plain English advice from a man they called *"Spag."* Spag was a retail legend. He took a less-than-modern facility, used uncommon marketing techniques and good old fashion "yankee ingenuity" and turned into one of the most successful one store retail operations in the country.

In the summer, to do business with Spag often meant going out back of his home office. There he would be on his hands and knees in his garden. I would ask a question about business or his health or just about life. Spag, often without looking up from the tomato plants he was planting would give a quick, yet sincere answer. There, in the garden, I was honored to be mentored by a legend…a legend with heart.

Jack Welch said *"Look for good ideas everwhere. Every time you find one, you've got yourself another mentoring experience."* Everyone you meet along your journey can be a mentor. They don't need a title or a big office. They might drive a Porsche or a Chevy. Young or old...black or white...doesn't matter. What matters is that you seek advice-guidance and wisdom that you can apply to make your success journey that much smoother…that much more meaningful and fulfilling.

I encourage you to pursue wisdom from others as you grow along in your success journey. I believe much can be learned from those who have gone before us. Some have become famous, and some not-so-famous. It doesn't matter. May the styles, wisdom and lessons from the following leaders assist you in finding the best leadership strategies for your career and for *your* life's journey.

PRESIDENT JOHN F. KENNEDY

"Leadership and learning are indispensable to each other" **John F. Kennedy**

In the early sixties, President John Kennedy set his sights on putting a man on the moon, and told the American people "We can do it!" He said it with such conviction that masses of people believed it, and committed themselves to making it happen. And, sure enough, in less than a decade, the first human being had walked on the moon. President Kennedy became one of our most beloved presidents, due in no small part to his leadership style and abilities.

LEE IACOCCA

"Where have all the leaders gone?" **Lee Iacocca**

Lee Iacocca stepped into the ailing Chrysler Corporation and said, "We are going to turn this company around!" With clear goals, a solid plan of action, and a strong conviction, he was able to inspire enough commitment from Congress to secure the largest loan ever made to a private company. Then he got the thousands of Chrysler workers believing in his vision and it enabled the company to pay back the loan ahead of schedule.

That's the formula leaders need to inspire commitment--clear goals, a solid plan of action, and a strong conviction. If you can communicate that to the people who work with you, you will have the kind of loyalty that makes them go the second mile...and beyond, if need be.

CAROLINE KENNEDY

"Ever since I was a little girl, people have told me that my father changed their lives." Now, Caroline Kennedy is a leader in her own right. With a Harvard diploma and her law degree from Columbia, Caroline has used her personal power to raise tens of millions of dollars for the New York City Public school system.

As a busy mom and best selling author, Caroline guards her time and privacy. She does, however, *make* time to use her quiet leadership style to assist the winner of the JFK Profile in Courage award, as well as the Commission on Presidential debates, the NAACP's Legal Defense and Education Fund, and to serve as an honorary chair of The American Ballet Theatre in New York City.

Caroline is proof that you can make a difference even if you exude a quiet demeanor and shun the spotlight.

JACK WELCH

"Leaders create a vision, articulate the vision, passionately own the vision, and relentlessly drive it to completion." **Jack Welch**

Jack Welch is a leader among leaders. The Financial Times named him one of the three most admired business leaders in the world. In *Winning: The Answers*, co-authored with wife Suzy, he offers some straightforward advice for a soon-to-be-grad. A college senior from California asked for help in choosing a career options. He was deciding whether to join a big company where he interned, or take a risk and join a start-up with friends.

Welch inquired why a twenty-one year old would ever "sign up to huddle in a corporate cubicle to do work you sort of like." He went on to advise this student not to do it to make parents happy, impress classmates or look good, but instead to "take chances, explore options and swing for the fences." Jack encouraged him to "take full advantage of what you have, a college degree, open mindedness to experiment, and permission to experiment and fail a few times."

In essence, Welch was advising to *take calculated risks,* give yourself time to identify your core values --that is what matters most, *then* you will be more prepared to become a leader in the appropriate envronment.

"Where is my perfect job?"

Like so many students, this young adult was looking for the smoothest path to greatness without taking any wrong steps or turns. They wish to identify the perfect job for them, even before they graduate. Jack Welch suggests that "You have to come to terms with the fact that most careers are not launched by a grand decision...and a clever game plan ...to get you there."

As stated above, leadership is a process. Each step positions us for the next in the process of becoming. Most careers do take unusual twists and turns. As much as we would like our success journey to be in the proverbial straight line, most times it doesn't work that way. Expect your journey to be a series of sometimes even and sometimes uneven steps. There will be times when your goals don't seem to line up with what your early vision for your career was.

I LIKE IKE

"You do not lead by hitting people over the head- that's assault, not leadership." **Dwight D. Eisenhower**

One of the great global leaders of the twentieth century was Dwight D. Eisenhower, 34th President of the United States. Before he became president, Eisenhower earned his stripes on the world stage during World War II. Growing up in Abilene, Kansas, he embraced the small town values that distinguished him for the rest of his life. Honesty, determination, and hard work were the foundation of his character. "Ike" became quite a scholar, as he saw education as a way to better himself.

Graduating from West Point in 1911, Eisenhower had a knack of saying the right thing to gain others' cooperation. His strong personality and overwhelming good nature inspired trust. Classmates regarded him as a natural leader who looked for ways to smooth over disputes and organize a group toward common goals. Thirty-three years after graduating from West Point, he was promoted to General of the Army in 1944.

Although he never saw action himself, he won the respect of front-line commanders. He dealt skillfully with difficult subordinates such as Omar Bradley and George Patton, and allies such as Winston Churchill and Charles de Gaulle. Whenever decisions on the battlefield were questioned, Eisenhower always took full responsibility.

He didn't pass the buck, blame a subordinate, or give excuses. He stood up like a leader and said: "I'm in charge. I will take responsibility for that action."....a timeless lesson for the 21st century leader to live by.

"Ike" became one of our countries most respected leaders and one of the most honored and decorated men in history. He received over fifty awards for valor, honor and leadership from twenty-five different countries.

JOHN D. ROCKEFELLER

"Good leadership is showing average people how to do the work of superior people."-**John D. Rockefeller**

John D. Rockefeller started Standard Oil at age 23. Through his empowering leadership style, Standard came to hold a virtual monopoly on the American oil industry. The company was so successful that Mr. Rockefeller became America's first billionaire.

Validating that leaders create an enduring ripple effect in the world, Rockefeller gave his money, energies and leadership to his favorite causes. He established charitable foundations and academic institutions, such as the University of Chicago, the Rockefeller Institute for Medical Research, a General Education Board, and the Rockefeller Foundation.

WARREN BENNIS

"The manager has his eye on the bottom line; the leader has his eye on the horizon." **Warren Bennis**

Warren Bennis, highly regarded as a modern leadership guru, identifies six qualities that consistently define a leader:

- **Integrity:** alignment of words and actions with inner values. It means sticking to these values even when an alternative path may be easier or more advantageous. A leader with integrity can be trusted and will be admired for sticking to strong values. They also act as a powerful model for people to copy, thus building an entire organization with powerful and effective cultural values.

- **Dedication:** spending whatever time and energy on a task is required to get the job done, rather than giving it whatever time you have available. The work of a leadership position is not something to do 'if time allows.' It means giving your whole self to the task, dedicated to success and leading others.

- **Magnanimity:** A magnanimous person gives the credit where it is due. They are gracious in defeat, allowing the defeated to retain their dignity. Magnanimity includes crediting other people with success and accepting personal responsibility for failures.

- **Humility:** The opposite of arrogance and narcissism. It's recognizing you are not inherently superior to others nor are they inferior to you. It doesn't mean diminishing yourself, nor exalting yourself. Humble leaders see all people as equal and know their position does not make them a god.

- **Openness:** being able to listen to ideas that are outside one's current mental models, being able to suspend judgment until after one has heard someone else's ideas. An open leader listens to their people without shutting them down early, demonstrates care; and builds trust and treats other ideas as potentially better than one's own ideas.

- **Creativity:** thinking differently, being able to get outside the box and take a new and different viewpoint on things. For a leader to be able to see a new future towards which they will lead their followers, creativity provides the ability to think differently and see things that others have not seen, and thus giving reason for followers to follow.

LEADERS LIVE IT...NOT JUST LEARN IT

"Leadership is practiced not so much in words as in attitude and in actions."
~Harold Geneen, Chairman, ITT Corp~

There's an old saying that pertains to leadership You've got to walk the walk, not just talk the talk. Put another way, you lead with the tongue in your shoes, instead of the tongue in your mouth.

Robert Thomas has done considerable work in the field of leadership. Leaving MIT to study business, union and political leaders on three continents, Thomas concluded that the most effective leaders practiced leading every moment of the day. He explains that "leading is not only what they do, it's who they are."

THE LEADERSHIP CHALLENGE

Leadership experts Barry Posner and Jim Kouzes created a research base of over 60,000 leaders. Their studies reach into all levels and in all types of organizations worldwide. In so doing, they unveiled recurring patterns of success and provided a solid, practical set of leadership concepts.

In their book *The Leadership Challenge,* they offer Five Fundamental Principles and Ten Behaviors within such principles for learning to lead.

Practices of Exemplary Leaders

Challenging the Process
• Searching for Opportunities
• Experimenting
Inspiring a Shared Vision
• Envisioning the Future
• Enlisting Others
Enabling Others to Act
• Fostering Collaboration
• Strengthening Others
Modeling the Way
• Setting an Example
• Planning Small Wins
Encouraging the Heart
• Recognizing Contributions
• Celebrating Accomplishments

Kouzes and Posner conclude that the extraordinary results achieved by ordinary people who apply these fundamental leadership skills validate the fact that "opportunities for leadership are available to all, ...and the only limits are limits we place on ourselves."

DO *SOMETHING*---MAKE IT HAPPEN

When all is said and done...when you have studied the various leadership styles and read the great advice from all the thousands of resources on leadership available, the bottom line is this:

- In order to be a leader, you must take action. It is not what the leader thinks that matters it's what he does.
- Leadership is influence, and all of us influence others intentionally and, most often, unintentionally.
- It's a responsibility.

You can be wise, mentored, polished, and prepared, but until you take action, you are not a leader, only a potential leader. Anyone can learn leadership skills, but learning isn't doing. Leaders don't just gather knowledge. They apply it. They do it. They live it. They make it happen. There are millions of potential leaders, full of advice and good intentions. But, where the rubber meets the road is when you get off of it and get on with it.

"Just as a compass points toward a magnetic pole, your True North pulls you toward the purpose of your leadership.

When you follow your internal compass, your leadership will be authentic, and people will naturally want to associate with you.

Although others may guide or influence you, your truth is derived from your life story, and only you can determine what it should be."

~Bill George, Author~
True North

Got Leaders?

❖ How would you define a leader?

_____

❖ Who would you say is a leader that you would follow? Why?

_____

❖ What leadership traits do you possess?

_____

❖ Which leadership skills do you wish to develop?

_____

❖ Do you see yourself as a leader? Why?

_____

MONEY
Make it--Grow it--Keep it

First, let me start off by telling you that I am not your one-stop shop for money advice. I have included this chapter after asking numerous educators, administrators and advisors what students need coming out of school. Most often, they answered money skills or money management.

According to surveys by The National Endowment for Financial Education, when it comes to finances, today's "twenty-somethings" are anxious about their finances. They report that sixty percent of those surveyed feel they face more financial pressure than past generations. In addition, thirty percent worry frequently about their debts.

Perhaps dedicating a chapter on this very important topic can help some of you *NOT* get behind the proverbial eight-ball financially. You will do much better if you develop a healthy relationship with M-O-N-E-Y.

From the time I was delivering newspapers in the project, I learned, not only how to handle money, but to respect it. It is a learned behavior that I truly encourage each of you to develop. You will work hard for your money. Invest some time to learn how to make money work for you. It will be worth it.

Now, let's get a couple things straight-

Number 1: Money is NOT the Root of All Evil

The Good Book doesn't say that. Look it up for yourself *(Timothy 6:10)*. What it does teach is "The love of money is the root of all evil...." Big difference. It was to me. I'll tell you why. When I began to make some "good money," I was told, by some that I was going to hell. That to pursue fame and fortune was wrong.

Well, at first, this bothered me. I mean, I was brought up a God-fearing, God-loving, church going guy (still am). If I knew that by trying to succeed and being compensated for it, I was doomed to eternal damnation, then I would have to make some changes.

I might either become a nun (I don't think so), or sell my houses and cars and live in a commune somewhere half way up a mountain. Now, I've got nothing against living off the land, or against nuns, for that matter. Actually, if it weren't for the 'good sisters' that taught and disciplined me, I might still be a smart-aleck project kid...only older.

Anyway, this fact cleared me for take-off. I was good to go. What I did realize was that my church, my alma maters and my favorite causes were glad...very glad, that I didn't go to the mountain and check out.

Number 2: Money by itself *WON'T* Buy Happiness

Just because you go out and make a bunch of it, does not guaranty you a life of bliss. Happiness is an inside job. No matter how big your bank accounts get, or, how luxurious your homes and cars, jets, or toys, to find true happiness, you must seek beyond external trappings.

Now, having said these two things, I want you to know that I am a big fan of prosperity. And there are many reasons for that. I am not going to list the many houses and fancy cars and world travel we've done to impress you, but I will say that I have been rich and I've been poor, and if you make me choose, I'm choosing rich.

Or, as a friend of mine said, "I've been with money and without it, and I conclude it's better to be with it." Same church...different pew. Another guy when asked how important money was replied that: "it was right up there with oxygen," which is quite important, wouldn't you agree?

Okay, enough of that, let's move on to how to make it and how to keep it. Most of us have been making money since we were kids. From various jobs, selling newspapers, baby-sitting, mowing lawns, etc. As soon as you go from it being handed to you, to earning it, money gains "value." In a very basic way, the value of money is in direct proportion to:

- **What you have to do to earn it**
- **What you have to give up to get it**
- **What you can do with it**

That's pretty basic. Yet, those same fundamentals hold true as we go along through life. Now, for me to tell you that money was never important to me would be a lie. It was. To a young city kid, having money meant NOT having to live in a small third floor apartment surrounded by blacktop for the rest of my life. It meant being able to buy a nice car, some nice clothes and go to Boston and see the Red Sox. Nothing wrong with those ideas, are there?--- Just some good, solid, All-American dreams, and all required money.

When you are in college, you just need enough to get by with a few extra bucks for pizza, a date, and to keep your car on the road. Yet, when you are looking out at "What's next... when I graduate," you realize that everything costs. Within six months of graduation, I had landed my first job in television, bought a new car and had a nice apartment.

I was "needing" more dollars for entertainment, expensive dates, and so on. It was not long after getting into the real world I realized I needed some basic financial planning or I was going to be broke for a long time.

10 MONEY TIPS FOR STUDENTS

Whether you are still in school, or have moved on, you will find these tips most helpful in getting yourself on firm financial footing. When you lived at home there are few financial decisions you have to make---how much to spend on food, essential bills like rent and electricity, and clothes and entertainment seldom cross your mind. In college, suddenly you have to consider these things. If you spend and spend you will quickly find yourself tapped out...*No fun.*

Smart money saving tactics can make a major impact on your finances and your future. They can also leave you with some left over to *have a life.*

The American Bankers Association Education Foundation offers ten tips to keep your finances from ruling your life.

1. Create a budget. To be fiscally fit you need to know how much goes in and out of your account. Keep monthly records of your spending and living expenses.

2. Get organized. Keep ATM transaction receipts, bills, purchases and tax records organized together in labeled files. This will help you stay on track with your budget and make it easier when it's time to pay bills.

3. Buy used books. Used books are usually in good condition and cost about half the price of new books.

4. Keep the car home. Parking, insurance, and theft are additional worries students can live without. More than likely everything you need is within walking distance.

5. Shop around. To get best prices, services, locations and lowest fees for credit cards and bank accounts.

6. Get smart about credit. Credit cards are not magic money; they're a loan with an obligation to repay. Don't spend more than you can afford to pay back.

7. Live within your means. Don't buy what you can't afford

8. Smart spending equals savings. Look for inexpensive ways to entertain yourself. Visit museums, parks, read at the library or a coffeehouse. Check out sales racks and search the internet. Do a little research, and save money.

9. Protect yourself. Don't be a victim of fraud or identity theft. Guard your credit card, PIN and account numbers.

10. Pay attention. Read your bills and statements. This helps you keep track of your spending, alerts you to fraud and any mistakes that may occur on your account.

KEEPING TRACK

To manage what you've got, you need to have a simple scorecard. We have found that inexpensive software can save you a lot of grief and money. The top two are Quicken (our choice), and Microsoft Money Plus. These user-friendly programs let you balance your checkbook, view credit card info, pay bills and manage investments online. They also offer upgrades for more advanced financial advice, such as tax prep and paying down debt .

MONEY MATTERS FOR THE NEW GRAD

Many of you coming out of school are carrying the weight of student loans. In addition, you may have picked up some of those "easy" credit cards along the way. The key to making your hard earned money grow is to find a system that works for you. Keep in mind, that one size does not fit all. Try a couple systems if you need to, but, please get one working for you as soon as possible. It can make the difference between being broke or financially solid in your latter years.

THE POWER OF COMPOUNDING INTEREST

Albert Einstein deemed the power of compounding as the Eighth Wonder of the World. Well, if this genius of a man saw compounding as such, we should pay attention. The power of compound interest is a simple savings plan that can help you grow your hard earned money. Let's start small and work our way up, shall we?

Suppose you contribute just $10 a week to an account that earns eight percent per year. That probably breaks down to one less pizza and soda per week. Not a big sacrifice, really. But, if you keep adding that little $10 faithfully, after twenty years, those ten dollar additions multiply into *over $25,000.*

Do it for ten more years and you've *got $65,000! Wow, that's a lot of dough!! And I don't mean pizza...*

If you double the amount you put away, your "nest egg" grows faster. Check out www.moneychimp.com for an online interest calculator. Have fun with it. See how high you can grow it. Then, set your goal, write it down and stick to it. The end result could be a fortune. It works, if you let it.

THE HIGH COST OF WAITING

Start putting away some money on a consistent basis ASAP. It's a fact, you can get by on just a little less and still enjoy life. The reality is, that if you make a habit of saving early on, you will gain a better quality of life for a longer time, both for yourself and your family.

*Check this out...*If you start saving just $50 a month at age twenty-five, you will have $175,700 at age sixty-five. *But,* if you wait until you are 45 and save that same $50 a month, you will only have a weak $29,500 at age sixty-five. Now, what do you think you're going to do with that little bit of money then? Not much...

POP QUIZ:

Which investment type produced the best returns over the past twenty years?

A) Savings Accounts
B) Stocks
C) Bonds

If you answered A, you are in the majority of 18-24 year old respondents, but you are incorrect. In a survey done by the PBS series *MoneyTrack,* their guess was savings (52%), bonds (20%), *then* stocks (16%). Stocks outperformed savings by 11 percentage points annually, bonds by 9 points. Ah, so much to learn...

AUTOMATIC INVESTMENT PLAN

Want to get into stocks and bonds, but don't have the know-how or the time to learn? Check out the automatic investment plan as your option for a savings system. Many mutual fund companies offer this plan. You decide how much to put in. Then, choose to either have that amount automatically deducted from your bank account, or mail it in on a schedule.

You can start with as little as $100. They do this with no transaction or broker fees, so the money grows faster. All of it can be done and tracked online, too.

They purchase mutual funds for you each time the money comes in. They do not try to time the market or pick what is hot and trade. They do what is called "dollar cost averaging." The best approach is if you can have it automatically taken out of your paycheck.

The old saying is you don't miss what you don't see. If it never lands in your account, you won't be tempted to spend it on what Robert Kiyosaki calls "doo-dads"--items that won't add to your net worth. A plasma T.V., the purse of-the-month, new Nike's...Get the idea?

INCOME PRODUCING PROPERTY

"Give me a lever long enough and a fulcrum on which to place it, and I shall move the world." **Archimedes**

In real estate, leveraging is the name of the game. Yet, you can only leverage what you have. This is a very good reason to keep your credit rating healthy. If you blow it, you reduce what you can leverage. Income producing, or rental property is what I used to grow my money.

How did I get into it, you ask? First, I did my homework. I read some books, and talked with some friends who had experience investing. I continued my education by reading the real estate classifieds, homes for sale magazines and speaking to realtors and a banker.

Finally, I took the plunge and bought my first piece. I borrowed some money for the down payment from a friend and leveraged my good credit and job income to qualify. It was a five-unit apartment house. You might say it was the ugliest house in a nice, middle class neighborhood. It was official. I was diversified. I had more than one income stream, which is a good thing.

I had heard many years ago that you shouldn't put all your eggs in one basket....*especially* if you don't own that basket. Why, you ask? Well, simply because sometimes they decide to "downsize" the basket. Other times, they will "outsource" positions. There are occasions when jobs are simply eliminated, or reduced to part time status. All of these unforeseen changes in a paycheck can make for tough times.

As you diversify, you develop a second income stream that can both get you through the rough spots, *and* grow to become a major source of income. So, I am a strong supporter of multiple streams of income.

Now, let me add an important principle here... I am a firm believer that as long as you are getting a paycheck from someone, you need to give them 110% when you are on their time. In other words, I do not advocate growing your investments or other source of income on the boss's time.

If you abide by this principle, you will be freed up to pursue whatever you wish on your time. I had a boss in television who attempted to take me to the task on my other ventures. While I respected his candor, I was able to respectfully point out to him that I was producing at the highest level in the department. In fact, they had never had one person produce so much business in their history.

However, I explained, once I leave here, it is my choice to go out and build a solid financial foundation for my family, while others decided it was more important to have "happy hour" with him. Now, I had nothing against him or "happy hours." My co-workers and I had a terrific rapport, as well. It was simply a matter of priorities and goals. I did not want to be a slave to the corporate world.

I was an entrepreneur looking to break out, willing to give up some social time now to buy my life back later.

A wealthy businessman once told me: "You make a living from nine to five, and you make a life after five." Great advice. I couldn't agree more. You can "get by" with what you put into your job. You can get wealthy with what you put into your spare time efforts.

BE YOUR OWN BOSS

In a survey by the Small Business Administration, 70% of young Americans said they wanted to own their own business someday.

In the follow-up survey, it was reported that 80% of them had no idea how they were going to do this. Well, in today's world, having a business of your own is easier than ever. You can choose a part time endeavor, such as a lawn service, baby-sitting, scrapbooks and the like.

If you are like many students, you have very little to invest. You might explore options such as a direct selling business. It is an industry that fits the 21st century economy. Numerous product lines ranging from health and wellness to skin care, cooking gear, it's out there. The keys to success in direct selling are to find products you believe in, and get involved with a support team who will train and coach you in your venture.

There are also online business opportunities to consider. Craigslist, for example, offers listings of people in need of services provided virtually. Ranging from graphic designers to personal assistants to you name it, it's available. So many choices exist that there are monthly magazines published solely for home-based businesses.

Often, a business is created from the talents a person has developed in school or at their job. Again, make certain you give your employer 110%, so you are freed up to provide your services outside of work.

Whichever path you choose, having a business of your own requires an investment. You either invest some money ...working capital, and/or you invest your time. You don't get *nuthin' for nuthin.'* In the end, if you're going to make some *real money* in your own business, you'll have to earn it! But, it's yours...*all yours*!

Be proud of your accomplishments. Each time you invest in yourself, you take a step toward financial independence...and that feels good! You are practicing "The Art of *not* having all your eggs in one basket." Let others spend their time and money foolishly, while you invest yours in your future. Smart choice.

BE A PLAYER

When it comes to money, I want to encourage you to get in the game...and play to win. I listen to so many people complain about not having enough money for this, we can't afford to do that, and on and on...

Having money is a decision, just like having a good attitude or writing down goals or going to college. It's your choice. You either *decide* to have it and keep it, or automatically default to not having it or blowing it.

I was born into a poor household, yet I *choose* to change that. I chose *not* to stay broke. I figured out that to change it, I must strive to succeed. Most people see the risk and turn away. They choose to stay average, and so does their income. To be above average you must get in the game.

Think about a giant football stadium. There are 70-100,000 seats surrounding a small green field. Down on the field, the "players" take care of business. They run and block and tackle, while the thousands of fans cheer them on.

As you watch the game, consider who is making the money and who is paying to watch them. Tens of thousands of people are paying to watch twenty-two professionals earn millions of dollars. When it comes to money, you must decide which place you want to be. Do you choose to be in the stands amongst the crowd, being entertained as life passes you by? Or, will you step up, learn a skill, become a professional and step on the field and become a player.

The spectators make lots of noise, while the players make lots of money. Your choice...

"To be a player, you must get in the game and increase your net worth."
~Uncle Dave~

Test Your Money Skills

❖ Do you consider yourself good with money?
   Why?   Why not?

❖ What type of investments do you have or intend to
   have? Why did you choose this type?

❖ Who has taught you about money?

❖ How do you protect yourself against fraud and scams?

❖ How do you plan on growing your money?

"If you don't take care of your money when you don't have much, you will NEVER have much."

~Uncle Dave~

BE ENTREPRENEURIAL
Think Like You Own The Place

*"The future will be owned and operated by
the entrepreneurial- minded."*
Mark Victor Hansen,
Chicken Soup for The Soul

They call this the Age of the Entrepreneur. We are living in a time when more and more people want to own their own business. Entrepreneurs and small business owners are responsible for 77 % of all the new jobs created in the past twenty years.

YOUNG ENTREPRENEURS AWAKEN

Studies have shown that right after college is an excellent time to begin an entrepreneurial career path. Some start while still in school. We will feature some of them here.

I was an entrepreneur before I could even spell it. Growing up in, I delivered newspapers everyday before school…weekends, too. It taught me the basics of owning and running a business. Those basics included:
-Handling money
-Being reliable
-Paying your bills on time
-On-time delivery
-Dealing with adults
-Overcoming challenges
-Developing a "whatever it takes" attitude

It is definitely a different mindset when you own something rather than just work for a paycheck. Though the responsibility falls squarely on your shoulders, at the end of the week, you get to keep more money. Why? Because, you treat it like a business-*your* business. Getting up early before school...through rain, snow sleet whatever, you do it. You take pride...the pride of ownership.

A business of your own is truly the Great American Dream. It is more attainable today than ever before! With online businesses and home-based businesses becoming more and more commonplace, there is no reason why a person who desires to have their own business can't have it.

ADVANTAGES OF OWNING YOUR OWN

Why do the majority of young people want to own a business? Here are some benefits of being The Boss:

- When you own it, you work smarter, not harder.
- You decide to concentrate on what brings the best return for your time and money invested.
- You get to keep more of what you make.
- You have job security, never worry about a "pink slip."
- You can start part time, keeping your regular pay until you can afford to break away.
- You start at the top, not the bottom.
- You work at your own pace and schedule.
- You can eat when you're hungry, not when you're told.
- You are free to work when and where you wish.
- You might even show up in your PJ's, if you'd like.
- You can work 'til dawn, sleep 'til noon and zip off to Hawaii without asking anybody for permission.

It is vital that you understand that building a sound, enduring, business venture takes time. If you dig below the surface of some "overnight success" stories, you find that they all paid their dues. It only seems like overnight to those of us not seeing the work they did in the trenches.

PREPARE TO FAIL—ARE YOU TOUGH ENOUGH?

Success requires mental toughness-a "Whatever It Takes" mentality. Are you willing to pay the price... to pay your dues... to persevere through the thick and the thin? 'The rich get richer and the poor get poorer." You have heard it a million times. Yet, my guess is that you have never heard it from the mouths of the 'rich.' Instead, this echo has most likely bounced to your ears with its origins being an excuse. That's right... an excuse. Excuses are what many use to pacify their guilt of not striving to reach their potential. A very wealthy man once explained to me: "Some people make excuses--Some people make money." You decide...I did.

THE SECRET

We all look for the one thing that will turn our idea, our dream, into huge success. There *is* a secret. Yet, it's only a secret to those who have not created that successful venture. What is the *secret*? The secret is to learn to invest your most valuable asset wisely...To treat it like gold. This asset is *more valuable than gold* And *if* you learn to value this asset as such, you put the odds clearly in your favor to make it...BIG.

Your most valuable asset is your time. You see, you are equally as wealthy as the richest men and women on the earth when it comes to time. Each of us gets the same amount-24 hours a day, 1440 minutes, 365 of them per year. You decide how you will treat that time. Will you spend it and waste it? Or will you invest it and multiply it?

Entrepreneurial-minded people seek ways to invest their time and multiply their efforts. The more you think like they think, the more you move toward becoming all that you are capable of becoming.

PROFILE OF THE ENTREPRENEUR

Sometimes it is hard to pin down a "typical" entrepreneur. They do, however, share many common characteristics. As you review the list, see how many of them you have. This will be a good indication if you are cut out to join the club of free market, enterprising, make-it-happen men and women.

ENTREPRENEURS:

- Are proactive
- Take calculated risks
- Are creative
- Are ambitious
- Are goal oriented
- Are persistent
- Are independent thinkers
- Are curious
- Are optimistic
- Are overcomers
- Go the extra mile
- Are self-confident
- Are dreamers
- Are innovative
- Are change agents
- Are people of integrity
- Are reliable
- Are competitive
- Are problem solvers
- Are flexible
- Are passionate
- Have a high energy level

How many of these do you have? This does not mean that you need ALL of these traits. No one has all of them, but the more of them you *do* have, the more you "fit" the entrepreneurial model. Remember, to be successful in your own business, you don't have to reinvent the wheel. If you can learn from those who have done it, and you'll be way ahead.

Learn from their victories and from their mistakes. There is no better way to prepare yourself for running a business, generate new ideas, and derive new insight than by examining the ideas, methods, proceesses, strategies, and recommendations of successful entrepreneurs.

Let's take a look at some of the most enterprising men and women of our times. As you read their profiles, see how many of the above traits you can identify.

Entrepreneurs

Sergey Brin and Larry Page
Founders, Google

Two most unlikely billionaires-Google co-founders Larry Page and Sergey Brin met while students at Stanford. Their $40+ billion empire does not restrict them from leading fun, yet simple lives. Both drive Priuses, the hybrid gas/electric car. They each "rent" modest apartments, work in casual clothes, and often break out for a volleyball game at lunch.

Each day, they come to play...er, work, at the GooglePlex, where there is a masseuse, a pool table, plenty of toys, scooters and bikes. Their culture *"work should be challenging and the challenge should be fun,"* seems to make the creatve juices of the Google team really flow.

What began as a research project in January 1996 has grown into an online force to be reckoned with. From a dominant search engine to online books, documents, Google Earth, Froogle, and more, their entrepreneurial culture has spawned enormous succuss. Though these two young men have accomplished so much in a short time, there seems to be so much more coming from this creative, innovative twenty-first century approach to doing business. Just a couple of loose, fun-loving entrepreneurs changing the world.

Thanks to Larry and Sergey, when we want to know about something or someone, we just *"google it!"*

Paul Tedeschi
CEO, Mr. Youth

It is said that out of adversity comes greatness. While Paul was still in grade school, his Mom realized that it was going to be a lean, cold New England winter for a single Mom raising three boys. Mom Judy called a family meeting and advised the boys that they were going to buy a chain saw and wood-burning stove to keep the heating bills down.

The boys would seek small jobs like shoveling snow and she was starting a business as the local "Plant Doctor." It was right there in those small steps of survival that the seeds of entrepreneurship were sown.

Paul took those "seeds" with him as he went off to college. As an undergrad at Boston University, carrying a full load of courses, Paul became the Advertising Manager for The Daily Free Press. From that, he and a partner began to venture into virtually uncharted territory doing marketing promotions *for* college students *by* college students, and thus Collegiate Advantage was born.

So, how did Paul manage to grow and run a multi-million dollar business and still graduate on time (four years, that is)? He did whatever it took. Getting up earlier than most would, and taking classes in the evenings so he could run the business during the day. Tasks like chasing clients, developing corporate promotions, vehicle sampling, and advertising campaigns for those looking to reach the valuable, but elusive 14-24 year old demographic.

Mr. Youth is a multi-faceted company. With their RepNation, they have created an ideal business model for young entrepreneurs. It provides students with the opportunity to have an income, learn how to run their own businesses, and associate with big-time companies as they participate in peer-to peer marketing.

Most importantly, it gives them a hands-on experience that no textbook or lecture can provide, thus preparing them to become skilled, seasoned, entrepreneurial minded and ready to transition as *most valuable players* in the real world. Paul's secret to success "Under promise and over deliver. Give clients more than they expect and earn their trust AND business for the long haul."

Rachel Ray
Everyday with Rachel Ray

Girl-next-door chef Rachel Ray seems to have come out of nowhere to enjoy a meteoric rise to the top. With *"30 Minute Meals"* on the Food Network, her own line of cooking gear, olive oil and cookbooks, she seems to have it all.

Well, it wasn't exactly overnight. Have you ever been in a store and gone by someone who is cooking up something and giving away free samples? Sure. We all have. Actually, there were times when we planned our trip so we could get there for "appetizers", then go off to dinner. *Are we the only ones who've done that?*

Rachel Ray started out doing just that... er, the cooking in the store part. Her in-store cooking turned into classes, which were noticed by the CBS television station in Albany, New York. She was offered a weekly cooking show, which she did for free for two years. She then got promoted to $50 per show for the next three years.

Rachel has taken her love of cooking and become an entrepreneur extraordinaire. From those beginnings working in a market and doing cooking shows for free, Ray has created a multi-million dollar empire. In typical entrepreneurial fashion, the affable Ray has used one successful venture (a cookbook) to grow a multi-faceted brand of ventures that have made her rich and famous.

She didn't do it because she went to the finest chef school in France (she didn't). Or because, she had drop-dead gorgeous, star-like looks. Rachel Ray built her success on traits typical of most successful entrepreneurs. Lucy Sisman, who was the design director of the magazine "Everyday With Rachel Ray" explains she did it *"through sheer hard work, application and cheer."*

Mark Zuckerberg
Founder, Facebook

When asked why he turned down the sale of his company or an estimated $30 Million, Mark Zuckerberg replied "I'm here to build something for the long haul." Zuckerberg started Facebook as a 19-year old undergrad at Harvard. He, along with roommates Dustin Moskovitz and Chris Hughes devised the roots of this most popular social network. Started as a networking site for college students, it has become a habit for over 20 million registered users.

Thefacebook.com, as it was originally called, was launched February 4, 2004. Within two weeks, half the Harvard student body had signed up and students from other colleges began approaching them, asking for online facebooks of their own. Within four months, they had opened up thirty schools. A STAR WAS BORN.

This tremendous trio started with a dream. *"We just wanted to make enough to go to California for the summer"* Zuckerberg stated. Well, that they did. And the rest, as they say, is history. He, too, lived in a rented apart ment sleeping on a mattress on the floor with minimal furnishings. The estimated value of Facebook is now over $3 Billion. *Ah, the life of a self-made billionaire.*

Stewart Butterfield and Caterina Fake
Founders, Flickr

When Stewart Butterfield first met Caterina Fake, he wowed her with his vision. He was a serial entrepreneur with a sparkle in his eye. Their first venture together struggled, then was on the ropes. Then came the idea for a photo-sharing website. And Flickr was born. They "bet the house," by taking out a second mortgage to keep their dream alive, their calculated gamble paid off. Less than eighteen months later, they sold Flickr for a rumored thirty million dollars.

Many entrepreneurs like Stewart and Caterina are glad to tell you that the road to success in your own business is not without risk. But if you persist, you have a chance at achieving your piece of the American Dream. Sometimes success does not come on the first try. But, the moral of the story is keep on trying until you make it.

Rueben Martinez
Founder, Latino Book and Family Festival

As a child, Rueben Martinez lived in a small town without a public library. His parents didn't read, still, Martinez developed a love of literature. Born the son of a Mexican copper miner, he became a barber in the Los Angeles area. Now Rueben is considered a genius.

In 2004, he became the first bookseller to receive a $500,000 grant from the MacArthur Foundation called "genius grants." It all began as a free lending library in his barbershop, where he lent copies of books to his customers. Eventually, he started selling books by Latino writers. By 1993, the book business had so outgrown its shelf that Martinez decided to put down his shears and turn the shop into a bookstore.

Rueben became a leading advocate of literacy and cultural education in the Latino community. He partnered with actor Edward J Olmos of *Miami Vice* fame to establish the Latino Book and Family Festival. It has become the country's largest Spanish book exposition. Martinez now has three stores generating nearly $1 million in annual sales. It was Rueben's spirit of serving and filling a need that has made him *"rich"* in more ways than one.

The Carney Brothers
Founders, Pizza Hut

In 1958, Frank and Dan Carney started a pizza parlor across from their family's grocery store. Their goal was to pay for their college education. Nineteen years later, Frank sold the 3,100 outlet chain called Pizza Hut for $300 million dollars. Carney's advice to aspiring entrepreneurs is to keep swinging. *"I've been involved in about fifty different business ventures, and fifteen were successful. That means I have about a thirty percent success average."*

The fact is no one bats a thousand. To be a success, you've got to keep going to bat and you will miss some, but you will get your hits, too. Hopefully a few home runs!

Maxine Clark
Founder, Build A Bear

After a successful corporate career, Maxine Clark decided to re-invent retail and make it fun her way! In 1997, inspired by her teddy bear, which was her best friend growing up, and the children in her life, she started Build-A-Bear Workshop to bring the fun back to retailing. Today, this concept, born out of a frustration with the way retail operated, has grown to be a multi-million dollar company with hundreds of Build-A-Bear stores across the U.S., and plans for several hundred more globally.

FROM FIRED TO ENTREPRENEURIAL WEALTH

J.K. Rowling: After being fired from her secretarial job, J.K. Rowling used her severance pay to help finance the first Harry Potter novel. She is the first billionaire writer.

Michael Bloomberg: lost his manager's job at Salomon Brothers, he sold his corporate stock and founded the Bloomberg Media empire now valued at $20 billion.

Bernie Marcus and Arthur Blank: Laid off in the late '70s, Blank and Marcus lost nearly $1 million the year they launched their first home-improvement store. Today, Home Depot has more than 2,100 stores.

David Neeleman: After Southwest Airlines bought David Neeleman's first low-budget airline, the company canned him as executive planner and he launched JetBlue.

INTRAPRENEURS

I am convinced that thinking like an entrepreneur will serve you well. Whether you start your own business or work for someone else, the mindset of being an owner is an invaluable asset. The term used for being entrepreneurial within a job structure is intrapeneuring ...or being entrepreneurial within an organization. Many forward-thinking companies are fostering this innovative, intrapreneurial way and seeing impressive results. After all, innovation is where change begins and true progress is made.

In his book titled *"Intrapreneuring,"* Gifford Pinchot defined intrapreneurs as *"innovative people within an organization who take ideas and turn them into profitable realities."* While so many of the characteristics of an intrapreneur are consistent with those of our typical entrepreneur, Pinchot points out a distinct difference.

When working within a structured, established organization, the innovator "must have the courage to do what needs to be done, even if it means bending or ignoring the rules." In the Intrapreneur's Ten Commandments, the first is "It is easier to ask forgiveness than permission." In other words, he suggests you "take the calculated risk, then say 'I'm sorry' and keep going."

So, yes, you *can* be an entrepreneur within a job structure, but be sure that the culture of the organization is not threatened by it. You must play by *their* rules if you want *their* paycheck. If you find that the culture is *not* conducive to your entrepreneurial style, you must either harness in your ways until you can move on to a better fit, or gradually change where you are by educating them as to the benefits of embracing the spirit of the intrapreneur.

Of course, you could decide to break out on your own and unleash the entrepreneur within…

ARE YOU READY TO BECOME THE NEXT YOUNG WEALTHY ENTREPRENEUR?

So, what separates these great success stories from the failures. Well, many quit when the going gets a little tough. Others decide that it's just too much work or taking too long to "make it." The difference, then, is not a matter of talent, or good looks, or the proper degree. The difference is in their persistence and focus and never-give-up positive attitude that achievers embrace. It's a choice. We either decide to follow our passions… follow our dreams, or we default to accepting others opinions and walk away wondering what might have been.

The moral of this story… Don't let anyone, any circumstance or any turn in the road, steal your dream. If you want it and it's real and it's good, then fight for it. Put aside anything that might get in your way and cloud your vision. Step over the shortcomings--- rise to the occasion.

Believe in the power of your dreams. If you always wanted to have your own business, go for it. Get some guidance. Model yourself after those who have done it. They know what it takes. Most of all, take action. The final mile of success is dependent upon your ability to apply the lessons learned. Nothing happens until you make it happen. Ralph Waldo Emerson said: *"What you do speaks so loudly that I cannot hear what you say."*

The Great American Dream is alive and well. Only you can decide if and when that passion is strong enough to make it come true for you. So, go on out and pursue your passion...follow your bliss. Who knows, someday we may be reading your success story right there along with Sergey Brin and Rachel Rays.

Hey, if they can do it, you can, too!

Test your E.Q. (Entrepreneur Quotient)?

❖ Do you consider yourself entrepreneurial? IF so, why?

_____

❖ Who do you know who is entrepreneur?

_____

❖ What's their strongest entrepreneurial characteristics ?

_____

❖ Is there someone who you would choose to model?

_____

❖ Which of the entrepreneurial traits do you possess?

_____

❖ If you could be any entrepreneur in the world, who would you be? Why?

_____

LESSON 401

ASSOCIATION
Who You Hang Out With Matters

"Statistically you will become the average and your income will become the average of the five people you associate with most!" **Jim Rohn**

I must confess. When I first heard the above statement, I was a bit concerned. I had just graduated from college and the people I associated with most were Heinie, Muggsy, Horseface, The Hick, and Colonel Puff... Now, I am not able to provide you with their average income, but perhaps from the names of these characters, you can see my concern.

Some twenty-plus years later, I can honestly tell you that I believe this statement to be absolutely true. *Who* you hang out with can determine *where* you will go. So, my advice is to choose your associates wisely. This, too, is a lifelong process. However, be aware that to deny this powerful truth is to risk the disappointment in not reaching your goals and dreams.

TRADE THE "IN" CROWD FOR THE WIN CROWD

*"Stop going with the flow in our life.
Start your own river instead."* **Dr. Phil**

At a Berkshire Hathaway Annual Meeting, a 14 year-old young lady stepped up to the microphone placed among the crowd of shareholders and asked billionaire Warren Buffett to share the keys to success. Mr. Buffett answered:

"It's better to hang out with people better than you. Pick out associates whose behavior is better than yours and you will drift in that direction."

GET AROUND THE RIGHT PEOPLE

Who are the right people to get around? Get around winners. Get around positive people. Get around people with goals and plans, people who are going somewhere with their lives and have high aspirations. Get around eagles.

Zig Ziglar says, *"If you want to fly with the eagles, you must stop scratching with the turkeys."* Get away from negative people. Get away from toxic people that complain and whine and moan all the time. Who needs them? Life's too short. Blossom-grow-become...

SEEK TO MASTERMIND

Napoleon Hill identified one of the principles of the super-successful: the concept of masterminding. The rich surround themselves with like-minded people, share ideas, learn from each other's experiences, and gained support and suggestions. The rich brainstorm and mastermind together. They sharpen steel on steel.

Your greatest asset going forward are the people around you and the people you are around. It is said that in the concept of masterminding, 1+1 does not equal 2. 1+1 equals 11. The collective ideas, thoughts and energies create a most powerful result. The finished product is far greater than any one contribution.

When developing a mastermind group, do not necessarily look for others who think just like you. A diverse group will bring more than all with the same viewpoint. With the expertise and experience of others, the seeds of an idea can be leveraged into an amazing finished product. You will gain different perspectives.

DEVELOP A LIBRARY

Develop a personal collection of books and CDs and DVDs filled with positive associations. There is such great power from that which we receive through our senses. Read, listen and watch that which will affect you positively. These have been my POWER TOOLS in changing my association to positive influences.

See our Resource section in the back of the book for some recommended sources. Go to our site for free updates. www.graduateandgrowrich.com

ARE YOU UNDER THE INFLUENCE?

The most profound influence from the outer world is other people The people you allow into your life and who you spend the most time with, are the greatest external forces as to the direction your life will take. Yes, external influences are *that* powerful.

You will be the combined average of the five people you hang around the most. You will have the combined lifestyle, health practices, thinking processes, expectations and income. Just think about it. Whatever and whoever are consistently in our space bring dominant thoughts, attitudes and actions to our reality.

Who we spend our time with determines what conversations dominate our attention and the observations, attitudes and opinions we are repetitively being introduced to. Eventually, we start to eat what they eat, talk like they talk, read what they read, treat people how they treat them, even dress like they dress and think like they think. All the while we might not even be conscious of it. And therein lies the danger...

Stephen Covey made a good analogy in his book *"The 8th Habit"*. He equates the unconscious influence of association to that of walking with a friend. When we walk with someone, we eventually and unconsciously end up matching their stride. If they walk slowly, we will slow down. If they walk briskly, so do we.

Have you ever been out to eat with a group of people who are more health conscious than you might normally be? Chances are you ordered something a little more healthy than normal? That is the power of associations; we are influenced to match their "stride". Unfortunately the same compulsion is true if you go out to eat with a group and everyone orders multiple drinks, heavier foods, desserts etc. This is also true of our attitudes, expectations, perspectives, beliefs, and opinions - in *every* area of our lives.

So, it is in your best interest to guard who you allow to control you through the influence of association.

DISASSOCIATION

There are people from whom you might need to break away from completely. This is not an easy task, but it is essential. You have to make the hard choice not to let certain negative influences affect you any more. First, decide the quality of life you want to have, *then* surround yourself with the people who represent and support that vision.

You may find this difficult, and even be ridiculed, but as we grow in life, we tend to change the circles in which we spend most of our time. This, in turn, fosters more growth, and most often association with others who are going in the same direction as we are.

NETWORKING

"If you build a network, you will have a bridge to wherever you want to go." **Harvey Mackay-Author**
What They Don't Teach you at Harvard Business School

As a student now is a very good time to begin to practice networking. Simply put, networking is exchanging information, resources and ideas in such a way that builds a relationship. To become a successful networker requires preparation, patience, persistence and practice. Just like friendships, some of the relationships that you forge will be short lived; others will last a lifetime.

You've heard the phrase, "It's not just what you know, it's *who* you know." The latest studies show that 65% of jobs in this country are either directly or indirectly gained through networking and personal contacts. Often such jobs are better opportunities with higher pay.

A vital concept to grasp is that networking isn't just about what other people can do for you. By thinking about how you can assist another person first, you will gain a following of people who will go out of their way to help you whenever the opportunity arises. Keep making new contacts, building relationships and have a system for organizing and keeping in touch with your contacts. It's a small world, after all, so keep your enemies to a bare minimum and NEVER burn bridges.

BEST PLACES FOR STUDENTS TO NETWORK

Alumni events, career days, family, friends, parents of friends, Chamber of Commerce events, clubs on campus, working professionals, and advisors. Reach beyond your comfort zone. Ask others to make introductions into the area you aspire to join upon graduation. Make the contact. Follow through, and *let the networking begin...*

10 STEPS TO POWER UP YOUR NETWORKING

Okay, you are going to a networking event. Here's what you need to know to make it worthwhile...and enjoyable.

1. **Mental preparation:** Ask yourself, *why are you going?* What do I hope to accomplish from this meeting-event? What do I have to offer this person? Successful relationships are mutually beneficial.

2. **Physical Preparation:** Dress appropriately for the event. Everything from your hair to your shoes are indicators of who you are. You never get a second chance to make a first impression. Oh, and don't forget the business cards.

3. **Smile:** Be friendly---everything else falls into place. People who smile are 100 times more attractive than people who do not. Friendliness breeds likeability. People do business with those they like and trust.

4. **Give a positive handshake:**---not a dead fish, weak handshake, and *not* a bone-crushing, "bring 'em to their knees" shake either. Make it firm, but not "killer." Your handshake projects your self-image in a way that breeds confidence.

5. **Make eye contact:** Look them in the eyes and think: *"I like you."* The positive are communicated. Your ability to look someone in the eye is a telltale sign of your own self-respect, as well as a display of respect for others. The eyes are the window to the soul.

6. **Listen:** We are born with two ears and one mouth. To grow successful relationships, use them in proportion. Be sincere. Reduce the "I, mine, and me." Increase the "you, your and yours."

7. **Find a common thread:** What's your common
    interest --kids, sports, hobby, club, charity?
    Ask questions like:
    *"What do you do in your down time? Married? Kids?
    What do you do for fun?"*

    Remember **FORM**: **F**amily, **O**ccupation,
    Recreation and **M**essage...or **M**oney

8. **Be upbeat and optimistic:** People are attracted to
    those who have a positive perspective. Leave the
    doom and gloom to others and stand above the crowd!

9. **Be complimentary and agreeable:** Not in a patroniz-
    ing way. Look for an opportunity to compliment
    someone sincerely. Develop an agreeable nature. You
    are much more likeable when you are agreeable.
    Then, let them know you agree with them...say so.

10. **Follow through:** An e-mail, a note or a phone call
    after your meeting acknowledging each person with a
    personal message referring to your conversation...the
    sooner and more personal, the better.

    Whom you choose to hang out with really does
    matter. I learned that every disassociation made room
    for new, dynamic, positive and influential associates. I
    developed relationships with new friends with whom
    we are enjoying life's journey.

    **Make the decision to associate wisely. Put yourself
    under the influence of Eagles ...And FLY!**

Associations

❖ Which of your current associates can you grow with?

❖ Where do you go to improve your networking skills professionally?

❖ On a scale of 1-10 (ten being highest), how good of a networker are you? Why?

❖ Which networking skills do you need to improve?

❖ Who do you know who you consider a terrific networker? Why?

CREATE A BALANCE
Body-Mind-Spirit

*"The way you think, the way you behave, the way
you eat, can influence your life by 30 to 50 years."*
~**Deepak Chopra**~

To live a balanced life is easier said than done. Most often, we are paying more attention to one part more than the others. To build a harmonious existence, we must find ways to nurture all three components of our being.

As you look at the three equally important facets of your self, realize that taking care of each one is essential for an enduring life of quality.

In my seminars, I will often tell the audience, "I know many of you want to be wealthy. Well, if you're going to be wealthy, you might as well be healthy." There's no sense in achieving your financial goal only to have your body fall apart from abuse or neglect, is there?

And if you are going to be healthy and wealthy, you might is well be happy, too. Do not neglect your soul…that inner you that needs to be fed. If you do that, all the money in the world will *not* make you happy.

Ron Hurst is a teacher, coach and operations manager. When asked what advice he would offer to soon-to-be graduates, Ron replied: "Embrace life holistically. Do not fall victim to a life of imbalance that will rob joy from you. In season imbalance is okay, but not as a lifestyle." Seek a balance to live a fulfilling life.

As you review this list remember that nobody does them all perfectly. Use them as a checklist. Give yourself credit for the one's that you do faithfully. Then, work on those areas that you know you need to improve. Set goals that are realistic, yet challenging. Now, let's explore some ways to accomplish this most important goal.

BODY

"The body is not a permanent dwelling, but a sort of inn, which is to be left behind when one perceives that one is a burden to the host." **Seneca (4BC–65AD)**

The body is the temple for our soul. Man's innermost desire is self-preservation. This is what I learned in school. For those reasons, I believe in taking good care of my body.

When I started traveling around the world, I really started to pay attention to how I treated my body. Believe me, there were many places I went to where I did *not* want to get sick and end up in a hospital.

The American Heart Association and the American College of Sports Medicine recommend that healthy adults engage in the following:

Either moderate intense aerobic exercise, such as a brisk walk for a minimum of thirty minutes a day five days a week, or vigorous intense aerobic exercise, such as jogging, for at least twenty minutes a day, three days a week, and 8-10 strength training exercises, 8-12 reps each, twice a week. Seek a physician's direction before starting anything new.

Basics for everyday well-being

Nutrition: Eat Well. Eat to live, rather than live to eat. -- just the opposite of what I did in college. I find I have a better consistent energy level and get sick less often. I've learned to read labels, seek a balanced diet, stay hydrated. And, don't forget your fruit and veggies...I also take nutritional supplements (vitamins & minerals). I think of them as cellular nutrition. They are infusing me with wholesome goodness from the inside out.

Physical Fitness: Take a walk, a run, park further away from the store. Join a gym. A combination of aerobic activity and weight resistance training is recommended. Take up a sport and stick with it. Develop a plan that works for you. Don't just sit there, DO SOMETHING!

Weight Control: Strive to maintain a healthy weight.

Safety- Live defensively, yet stay optimistic. As I told my son as he started driving, *"Watch out for the other guy."*

Say NO to Toxins: Get away from toxic environments, whether you ingest them or associate with them. Avoid them like the plague. If they're not good for you, ban them.

Appearance: Maintain good grooming, hygiene and dress. As the old saying goes *"If you look good, you feel good. And you look marvelous!"*

Preventative Health: Don't wait until you're sick. Seek care and direction regarding family history, genetics and environmental exposure.

Manage Stress: Stress can do a number on your body. Seek counsel or professional advice as needed. For me, it's consistent exercise. The World Health Organization estimates 80% of illnesses are directly or indirectly caused by stress. So, if you're not proactive in busting stress, it's likely to come back and bust you!

"Be good to yourself. If you don't take care of your body, where will you live?" **Kobi Yamada**

MIND

Formal Education: Complete your formal education. You've come this far.

Lifelong Learning: Seek programs to continue your education. Often these are made available through your employer. There are numerous opportunities for skill development, too. By all means, take advantage of what is offered. It keeps you sharp, informed and competitive in the workplace. There's always so much to learn.

Avoid Negative Saturation: Limit your intake of the barrage of bad news. There is more media today than ever before. Your mind can be totally saturated with reports of war, crime and adversities. Protect your mind and your sanity. Control your daily intake of this information. It can be detrimental to your outlook on life.

Read: Read in a variety of areas. I like sports, business. and biographies of people I admire. Whatever you enjoy or have a passion for, read to feed your head good stuff to offset some of the bad news.---Ladies, not just a saucy novel. And guys, the glossy magazines with lots of pictures, even if you say you buy it for the articles, are not exactly feeding your mind good stuff. Open up and put some good stuff in there.

Music: I love music, all kinds of music. It relaxes me. It gets me moving when I'm in the gym. It keeps me awake when I'm driving late. It is inspirational. I reminisce to it. Music is good for all three, really, mind, body and soul.

Visual Input: Good movies...Some of my favorite are Rudy, Sea Biscuit, all the Rocky flicks. I also enjoy Biography, The Food Network, PBS...mix it up!

Words: Your words matter. Speak pleasant words-words of life, encouragement, and thanksgiving. The Good Book tells us pleasant words are healing to the body. Listen only to pleasant, life-giving words. Choose life by choosing life-giving words and you will see a divine healing operating in your life. You'll feel strength and peace in your soul that will move you into an abundant life.

SPIRIT

Be a seeker of greater spirituality. Cultivate that peaceful place within you. Quiet the noise--Still the body. Allow the inner you to rest. Some do it through prayer, others with meditation, yoga, soothing or music. Perhaps, a warm bath with candles, low light and a quieted mind (my wife's favorite). The idea is to get away from it all, while melting *into* the serenity of it all.

Explore the many possibilities. Find one or more that work for you. This becomes essential to your overall well-being. To feed the body and busy the mind without quieting and connecting the soul makes for an unbalanced person. It shuts out the quiet, calm connected spiritual side within a living person.

The Grand Canyon is not an everyday sight, but it certainly is awe-inspiring. It's an extraordinary time-stopping experience, a "WOW" moment. Enjoy them when you experience one. They don't come along all that often.

Yet we should go through life each day being aware of mini-wow's in our everyday path. It does not always have to be a large block of time to be effective. Sometimes, it's just taking a moment to enjoy a sunrise or sunset, to cherish the innocence of a small child enjoying the ducks on the pond, or the incredible color of the trees changing color right before our eyes in autumn.

I have found that it doesn't take any time to stop and smell the roses of life every single day. It is mostly an awareness --- an appreciation for the beauty around us. It is, indeed, more valuable to our inner soul to quiet the noise and enjoy life's little wonders than to just let the onslaught of the in-your-face elements of the world sap our inner joy.

Seeking an effective way to balance the "crazies" is most important for us to be happy along the way. It's not the easiest thing to do. Between school, work, studies, relationships, and so forth, life is busy. We are burning the candle oat both ends...on the go, night and day. We may ask the question *"Who am I? Why am I here? Am I more than hair, eyes, nose, and mouth?"*

"I'm just a bundle of things inside of myself that I don't know. I am fear, anger, and distress all the time. I feel depleted. Whenever someone asks me to do something for them, I hardly have anything to give because I am running on empty all the time."

Many feel this way. When you're in school, at times you work so much that you feel depleted. You wonder, *"How will I get through another day? Where will I find the wisdom to pass this test?"*

You have a spiritual power that is beyond your power as an isolated human. When you tap into that inner power, you will be burning with a full flame, a higher flame, a brighter flame. You are being recharged, and you are continually causing the flame to glow. It never burns out. It's always there to help re-balance the whole you.

The secret is to find how to tap into it. What does it for you? For me, it's reconnecting with my maker. Wherever I go, wherever I've been, I've always been able to find a sacred place to stop for a few minutes and pray.

I've stopped and reflected inside awe-inspiring "duomos" in Italy, a little, tiny grotto in the Swiss Alps and a chapel by the sea. They all work for me. Just a few minutes of quiet and solitude, in prayer, and I am recharged and ready to go. The key is for you to find what works for you.

RECONNECT

Judeo-Christian principles teach the importance of balance in the big picture of life. One of the Ten Commandments states to *"remember to keep holy the Sabbath."* Wisdom gained through the ages confirms that one day in seven, we should relax, retreat and regroup. Take the time to review and reload.

We get refreshed, reconnected and ready to re-enter. As we refill our physical, mental and spiritual fuel tanks, we equip our *TOTAL SELF* for the next step on life's journey.

STUFF HAPPENS

Do you remember when we were children what we lived for? We lived for joy. Every second of every day was full of carefree joy. But something happened to us. Work happened to us. We go to work with great excitement saying to ourselves, *This is going to earn me money so I can have more fun. I will be able to do the things that I've always wanted to do. I can take those trips. I can buy that car. I can do all the things I've dreamed of.*

Goals and dreams and wanting to succeed are fine. However, when they pull us out of balance, they can stress us out, and become counter-productive to our being a "success-full" person. Without feeding the spirit, we are clearly out of balance and often, emotionally out of control. It is essential to constantly be moving toward a balanced life

Putting all your eggs in one basket and expecting to come out whole and healthy is irrational is destructive thinking. We all need to perceive a world larger than the small world of our work. We must nurture our private selves as well as our professional selves. Seek to increase your spiritual time to find that healthy balance, which is essential for us to live happy, fulfilling lives.

A LESSON FROM THE OSTRICH

The most misunderstood animal in the world is the ostrich. People think the ostrich puts his head in the sand to hide. But actually the ostrich is hard of hearing and puts his head in the sand to tune into the vibrations of what's happening around him.

When we go apart for a while to re-connect, we are not putting our heads in the sand to hide. We are tuning into the spiritual vibratory force that will come through us, renew us, recharge us, and help us to go about our daily living fully alive. Frankly, I don't know how people find inner peace and harmony within their lives without this constant connection.

FLOWER POWER

My wife is an amazing gardener. I continue to learn, but she is miles ahead of me. Over the years, I have come to appreciate so much of what flowers have to offer us as humans. The colors, the sizes, the birds they attract, and certainly the fragrances they bring. Pleasing to the senses and brightening up our days!

There is something about looking at a spray of flowers, particularly in the dead of winter, that reminds us that "this too shall pass", giving us the extra little nudge to look forward to the future. Perhaps that's why flowers have been shown to improve depression in people.

In fact, the health value of flowers is not simply my opinion. Several interesting studies show the power of the flower. In *Eight Weeks to Optimum Health,* author, Dr. Andrew Weil recommends purchasing flowers regularly to reduce stress and bring beauty into your life. Scientific evidence has shown that receiving flowers lifts our moods. *Evolutionary Psychology* reported the results of three studies showing the positive effects of flowers.

- Women smile virtually every time they receive them.
- Both women and men smiled genuinely and initiated conversation when given a large Gerbera daisy.
- Men and women 55 or older who receive flowers show improvement in mood and cognitive function.

The conclusions are clear: cultivated flowers bring out positive emotions in humans, and with positive emotions comes health and longevity. Flowers are a simple and inexpensive choice for to improve both happiness and health no matter what the world outside looks like. So, whether you are giving them, receiving them or just buying some for yourself, there is power in those flowers.

SMILE

If you want people to be friendly and open toward you, you must be the same toward them. The first visible sign of such openness is a smile. Laura Lewis, the author of *52 Ways to Live a Long and Healthy Life,* says smiling is more than just dazzling people with a pageant puss worthy of Miss America. A smile, it turns out, is more than skin-deep. *"If you smile, your body will think you're happy,"* Says Laura, *"and respond accordingly." "When you smile, you contract 42 facial muscles. This constricts and slows blood flow to the brain via your sinuses, thus cooler blood reaches the hypothalamus – the master controller of body temperature and emotion. The result: more pleasant feelings."*

LIGHTEN UP

"Humor is the sunshine of the mind." **E. G. Bulwer-Lytton**

Laughter is equally therapeutic. Did you know that laughing 100 times during a 24-hour period provides the same cardiovascular benefit as working out on a rowing machine for 10 minutes? Here's how it happens: When you laugh, your blood pressure and heart rate rise. Afterward, they drop lower than they were before the hilarity. Moreover, because laughter accelerates your blood flow, you have more ammo to repel infection and disease, you feel less pain, and levels of stress-induced hormones (such as epinephrine, cortisol and dopamine) fall. The lesson is obvious: Smile and laugh often for the health of it. So do as Tony Bennett says: *"Put on a happy face!"*

WHAT'S YOUR PRIORITY?

You've decided to make your health a priority in your life. You're going to work out regularly, eat right, manage your stress. There's one problem- - what about all the other priorities in your life? You can't help wondering if your work, family, social or personal life will suffer from this time-consuming new commitment to healthy living. After all, there are only so many hours in the day.

The problem is a realistic one that most people face, says Minneapolis lifestyle coach Kate Larsen. "Our lives are so busy with various demands and commitments, that – sadly - it is common for healthy habits to get lost in the shuffle. When we decide to make our health a priority, we usually have to change our whole way of life, including our priorities and our attitudes."

The first step to changing your priorities is to assess your existing ones. If you have no personal time to begin with, you may resent a fitness program before you even start. If your family and friends are currently neglected, adding a new commitment is bound to cause resentment. After you have assessed your out of balance areas and determined ways to correct them, your healthy new habits will have a much better chance of surviving.

"Sometimes I don't even like to use the word balance," says Larsen, "because people think it's a permanent, achievable state of being. It isn't. Living a balanced life is like surfing. It's always changing. You ride the waves of circumstance and try to stay balanced, but you're going to get knocked off your board and go under sometimes. That's part of life: Just get back up and try again."

How do you balance new habits with the rest of your life and make sure they remain a top priority? Larsen offers the following guidelines:

Write It Down: Write daily, weekly and monthly goals in your journal, planner or computer organizer. Schedule your priorities: fitness time, grocery shopping, meal prep, relaxation and family time. Writing things down helps build awareness and increases (but doesn't guarantee!) your chances of following through.

Think "No Matter What . . ." For each day, week and month, plan the priorities that you put in your "No Matter What" category: *"I will exercise no less than four times this week, no matter what,"* or *"I will take at least 20 minutes of quiet personal time each day, no matter what."* Remember that you already have many activities that are "no matter what." Would you go a week without brushing your teeth, or only getting four hours of sleep each night? You want to think about your new healthy habits in the same way.

Set Rules: Your life slides out of control and your priorities go haywire when you don"t set boundaries. (If the idea of "rules" scares you, think of them as gentle guidelines.) Set the number of nights you will allow yourself to be away on business travel, the number of overtime hours you will work, when you will and will not answer the phone and e-mail, how often you will entertain, how many hours of sleep you will get, etc. Of course, some circumstances may create exceptions and you need to be flexible. But guidelines will give you a standard for making decisions that align with your values and goals.

Create "Sacred Time." Create pockets of time that you will not allow to be compromised by any other obligations. For example, "Every Friday night is family activity night," or "6:00 to 6:30 am is my time to relax, read and meditate."

Much of life is about the balancing of two opposites; like the positive and negative charge on a battery. Life's balancing of opposites totally surrounds our lives— man and woman, day and night, good or evil, life and death, water and land, joy or sorrow, summer and winter, contraction and expansion. As you constantly seek a balance in your life, be sure to take time for all that is important.

TAKE TIME

Take time for work, it is the price of success.
Take time to think, it is the source of power.
Take time to play, it is the secret of youth.
Take time to read, it is the fountain of wisdom.
Take time to be friendly, it is the road to happiness.
Take time to dream, it is hitching your wagon to a star.
Take time to love, it is the highest joy of life.
Take time to laugh, it is the music of the soul.
~Anonymous Irishman~

Balancing Act
❖ Rate yourself in each of these vital areas:

	Honors	Passing	Failing
Family			
Fitness			
Friends			
Nutrition			
Finances			
Spiritual Life			
Fun/Pleasure			
Personal Growth			
Professional Life			
Relaxation/Recharge			

❖ Which area of my life could most use re-balancing?

❖ What specific things can I do to correct the areas that are out of balance ?

❖ How will I integrate my planned changes with other priorities in my life?

GIVING BACK
Make A Difference

"When you have done well, send the elevator back down." **Jack Lemmon, Actor**

What great advice! Giving back is about serving others. As we stop and count the many blessings in our lives, it is clear that what shapes our brand is directly related to how we can make a difference; Small ways--big ways--they all count, and they all *do* make a difference. The mere act of serving others with whatever capacities we have is a humbling, enriching experience. You cannot serve others without receiving great return on a very personal level.

"I don't know what your destiny will be, but one thing I do know: the only ones among you who will be really happy are those who have sought and found how to serve." **Albert Schweitzer**

BECOME A PERSON OF POSITIVE INFLUENCE

During our lifetime, we all develop a sphere of influence. Beginning with our immediate family, continuing with our classmates, peers, co-workers, and so forth. We influence others by the mere fact that we exist. We are in the same space as they are. We have shared inter-ests--likes and dislikes--common relatives and more.

We, by our actions and how we live our lives, influence their lives. This influence can either be good, or not so good. Decide that your influence will be good. Somebody is always watching. It might be your kid brother or little sister. It could be a friend who is quietly seeking a role model, which may determine if he or she makes good choices or poor choices about their future.

As you move along in your journey, your potential influence can become wider. Perhaps it spreads to a blind person, an under-privileged family, even to a third world country.

We have been blessed with the opportunity to adopt two beautiful children. My daughter Noelle was born in Korea. She had been left on the doorstep of an orphanage in Seoul—abandoned—by a mother who made two decisions.

The first decision was to give her life, rather than not have her. The second decision was to give her up, hoping and perhaps praying, that someone would take her and nourish her, keep her alive. She hoped that this little helpless baby would have a better life, which she was unable to provide. We are so thankful she made both of those decisions.

Years later, my wife Linda and I traveled to Korea to speak at a large business conference in Seoul. We had such a wonderful time. Great food, beautiful country and wonderful people! We found the Korean people to be hospitable, caring, intelligent, and ambitious.

As we enjoyed an elaborate nine-course traditional Korean meal, several in our dinner party became most interested in the fact that we had a Korean daughter. After the meal, our escorts continued this interest as we returned to our hotel.

In confidence, the couple shared a heart-stopping truth with us. They explained that in Korean culture, if a baby girl is born out of wedlock, her origins unclear, her life is lived as a social outcast. No one will claim her. No one will advocate for her. She goes it alone. In most cases, she lives on the streets---*abandoned—for life.*

Well, I must tell you, that was a reality shock for us. Time stood still at that very moment for me. I cannot tell you that when the decision was made to seek an international adoption, that we knew the fate of young girls in Korea, such as Noelle. We did not. But to the core of our soul, we knew going through the expense and time and difficulties that it took during the process seemed so minute compared to the influence we could have on one very special girl's life.

Peter McClintock, a good friend of mine, has a favorite saying. He believes that these things are not coincidences. He prefers to call them "God incidences." Peter, I couldn't agree with you more. Noelle was meant to be and she was meant to be my daughter. And that, my friends, was no coincidence.

My son was born in the Philippines. Josh is a very bright young man. He is enthusiastic, loves life and is full of dreams. I will never forget returning to the Philippines on business. I found the Filipino people to be so pleasant and friendly. Their spirit is joyful, and contagious. Yet the reality of what would have been slapped me in the face this time.

The taxi was traveling around Manila. Beyond the bright hope-filled faces, you notice the poverty. These conditions we seldom see here in America. Amidst the thick, heavy pollution, clean laundry hung over an alley to dry above a dusty, unpaved roadway.

Now picture this. Throughout the streets, wherever we went, young boys and girls were selling gum or some small trinkets …even themselves, I was told, to bring home a few dollars so their families could survive.

As the car pulled up to a stoplight, a little boy, about the age of my son, hurried over to our cab. He flashed a big, beautiful smile and asked if we would like some gum, or our windshield washed, or anything?

Now, I am sure that my taxi driver was pretty used to this scene. After all, he lived there and made a living driving amongst these young people every night and every day. He probably didn't even see the young boys sparkling eyes and hopeful smile. But, I did. And, once again, time stood still.

This was not just a boy in the street. It could have been my son Josh. He looked just like him, that beautiful smile and sparkling eyes on that shiny brown face.

And I just sat there with tears streaming down my face, unashamed. I was thankful that we had the opportunity to influence another bright shining star in the person of Joshua Bedard. It was, indeed, another God-incident of immense proportions!

HOW CAN STUDENTS MAKE A DIFFERENCE?

"You are not here merely to make a living. You are here in order to enable the world to live more amply, with greater vision, with a finer spirit of hope and achievement. You are here to enrich the world, and you impoverish yourself if you forget the errand."
~Woodrow Wilson~

Perhaps you are thinking, "Well, I'm not rich, nor am I famous (yet). So, how can I, in my present circumstance, make a difference? It's just little old me, you know."

There are so many great causes where you can get involved. There are two ways for you to contribute. Either, be a volunteer or be a philanthropist. Rather than decide for you, I'll leave that for you and your personal situations.

When Hurricane Katrina hit, it's fury and after-effects reached all of us. My daughter was nineteen and my son was seventeen. Both were students and worked part-time at a fast food restaurant. We had a family meeting to discuss what we could do to reach out to those whose lives were turned upside down by this mighty storm. These two young teenagers decided to give up what equated to a weeks pay apiece and send it to the Red Cross to assist their efforts. *They decided* to believe that they could make a difference.

As you saw the enormous destruction left by Katrina, you may have been inclined to think "It's hard to believe that my little donation makes any difference." Yet, if everyone felt that way, hundreds of millions of dollars would not have flowed toward to relief efforts. Fortunately, so many overcame their own feelings of doubt and sent it in anyway.

Perhaps reflecting on the lyrics from Martina McBride's song *Do it Anyway* is just the right stuff for us to remember when doubt creeps in:

> *"This world's gone crazy*
> *And it's hard to believe*
> *That tomorrow will be better than today*
> *Believe it anyway."*

Tomorrow will be a better day for not only us, but for those to whom we reach out and give a little of ourselves to, thus *making* it better than today in some small way.

LIFE'S A BEACH

I am reminded of one of my favorite beach stories. My wife and I lived right on the beach for almost 10 years. Our fondest memories are of waking up and having our morning coffee on our balcony overlooking the beauty of the ocean. So often, we would enjoy dolphins as they playfully moved along just steps from the shore. Ah, such is the beauty of dreams come true. Back to my favorite beach story:

A young couple is holding hands while walking the beach, just going along in the surf and enjoying the unique beauties of where the sea meets the sand. Looking ahead, they noticed an older man. He was routinely picking something up and tossing it into the water.

As they got closer, they saw exactly what he was doing. Along the edge, there were hundreds of starfish, which had washed up on to the shore. This old man, who did not bend over as easily as he was once able to, just kept picking up one starfish at a time and tossing them back into the water. As the young man approaches, he asks: "Old man, why are you spending all your energy tossing those starfish back into the ocean? Can't you see all of these starfish? There are way too many. Do you think your efforts can really make much of a difference?"

As the young man finished saying all of this, the old man reached down and picked up one more starfish and gave it a toss back in to the water. As he completed this toss, he turned to the young man and simply said: "It made a difference to that one."

Sometimes we don't think our small efforts make any difference. Let me assure you, they do. It may not be saving a life, ending world hunger or stopping a war. But, believe me, we make a difference... one starfish at a time.

NAVIGATORS

There's a destiny that makes us brothers.
No one goes his way alone.
All that we send into the lives of others,
Will come back into our own.   **Edwin Markham**

My niece, Lauren decided to make a difference between semesters. She joined up with an on-campus group called the Navigators. The Navigators have been investing in people for more than seventy years. An interdenominational non-profit organization with outreach programs in more than 100 countries, the Navigators are teaching college students how to give back as a part of their educational experience.

She signed on to go to the Philippines during her summer break with the objective to help out in the school, the orphanage, and the medical clinic. Having never been that far from home, let alone being immersed in a third world environment, we spoke about the people and the overall climate in Manila and its surroundings. I shared with her how we had found the city quite hectic, smoggy and noisy. Yet, the Filipino people were so warm and happy and welcoming in spite of their living conditions.

Lauren had a life-changing experience. She explained how she had enjoyed being a part of this culture so different from her normal environs. She continued: "Living in the squatter village helped us form relationships with the people as well as realize how blessed I am." She and her fellow Navigators experienced many heartfelt moments including "witnessing the birth of twins who had been expected to die and assisting in the surgery of a deformed boy." While living quarters were far below what they were used to, these students were impacted by such simple things as "helping to build a shower and sink with clean water where none had existed and establishing a dental office, where there had been no toothbrushes."

I particularly enjoyed seeing pictures of Lauren holding a playful, spirited little boy who was not feeling deformed, but appreciative of the love and care given by some college students from far away.

Lauren simply referred to her trip as *"amazing experiences that I will never forget."* I can't help but think that the memories that Lauren and the other Navigators hold dearly have made them "Grow Rich" in ways that most "spring breakers" will never know until *they* grow...and go.

NASCAR STAR GIVES BACK

Jeff Gordon is a Big-Time winner on the race track. He is a perennial top money winner, yet it is his off-track generosity that makes the most difference.

The Jeff Gordon Foundation was founded in 1999 to focus on what was becoming an endless list of causes Jeff wanted to help. It came down to the two that had affected him so deeply: blood diseases and kids.

"Whether it's meeting a Make-a-Wish child or providing financial support for hospitals, he applies the same intensity to the foundation that he does to racing. "You want to help everyone, but that's impossible," he says. "You have to focus on what is closest to your heart."

Giving back to mankind, leaving your place, your space, your world, a little better than you found it...that is what giving back is all about. If you will count your blessings each day, you will truly know in your soul that the only way to say thank you is to pass on a little hope to someone else.

And, please, don't wait until you're old and retired to make a difference. You can encourage someone everyday. How? With a smile, a kind word, a compassionate ear to listen, a sincere "nice job."

Beyond that, I am certain that each and every one of you can make a bigger difference simply by deciding to give of your talent to a worthy cause or donate some hard earned money to something or someone you believe in.

GIVING BACK WISDOM

Mitch Albom is the author of one of the greatest, most touching books I have ever read called *Tuesdays with Morrie*. Mitch shares the life lessons he learned from his college professor Morrie, as he is lay on his deathbed.

Here is a small sample of these invaluable lessons:

- *"The way you get meaning into your life is to devote yourself to loving others, devote yourself to your community around you, and devote yourself to creating something that gives you purpose and meaning."*
- *"The most important thing in life is to learn how to give out love, and to let it come in."*
- *"So many people walk around with a meaningless life. They seem half-asleep, even when they're busy doing things they think are important. This is because they're chasing the wrong things."*

What would you be giving back if were you in your last days? Get this book. I've shared it with some of my closest friends, including my wife, Linda. It's a life-changer.

GIVING BACK—YOUR CAPSTONE PROJECT

"Volunteers do not necessarily have the time; they just have the heart." **Elizabeth Andrew**

As you complete your degree and prepare to graduate, you must summarize your academic experience. Unlike your formal education, this capstone project does not have a time limit. You are able to begin it while still in school, yet you may continue it for as long as you wish.

Now's a good time for you to think about how you would like to be remembered. How will you give back?

Mahatma Gandhi said: "My life is an indivisible whole...all my attitudes run into one another; ...they all have their rise in my insatiable love for mankind."

Where does your insatiable love lie? Is it totally selfish? Or will you develop it to become self-less? Your ability to do so will determine your legacy...your giving back quotient.

I have found my giving back has grown, changed directions and provided innumerable returns through the years, many of which are intangibles. From putting a few nickels and dimes in a poor box to sponsoring scholarships, serving on college boards and the Junior Achievement organization, it's been a diverse ride, so far.

Yet, my capstone project is still not complete. I vow to continue to strive to make a difference until they put me in a box, hopefully many, many years from now. Even then, it is my hope and dream to have infected my family, friends and all that I can, with the spirit of serving and giving back.

The secret of living, my friends, is giving. You can grow no richer than to earn a position where you can make a difference with your talents. As you identify those who can benefit from your "riches", and devote yourself to pouring it out so that others can "GROW RICH."... It is when your giving back excites you, stirs your soul and lights a fire within that you have GRADUATED....*WITH HONORS.*

"It is one of the greatest compensations in life that no one can help another without helping themselves." **Ralph Waldo Emerson**

SIX WAYS A STUDENT CAN GIVE BACK

- Volunteer at a school: Coach, tutor, read a book, be a coordinator. Call your local school or contact Junior Achievement: www.JA.org.

- Donate a skill: Everyone is good at something-helping at a bake sale, bookkeeping for a non-profit or swinging a hammer. Contact Habitat for Humanity www.habitat.org

- Be a visitor: Nursing homes, hospitals, a relative who is ill or homebound. Animal shelters welcome visitors to play, wash, feed or care for the animals.

- Provide transportation: Many people are not able to drive, so step up and help. Drive a senior to the doctor's office, or take a neighbor to church.

- Collect/Sort/Deliver goods: Organizations and shelters often need help to sort and organize or deliver. Contact your local church, a shelter or Goodwill. www.goodwill.org

- Donate blood: It is truly the gift of life. You can help an accident victim, people undergoing surgery, a cancer patient. There are so many in need...you can save someone's life.

So, come on...Graduate.
Then, come out and make a difference.
We'll be there waving the checkered flag for YOU!

The Last Word

It is my hope that this Guide is a help to all who read it. After more than twenty-five years in the "real world," my return to life on campus was quite the eye opener. Finding bright, wide-eyed, ambitious men and women who want to know what they need to be successful has been the "wind beneath my wings" in offering the life lessons in this book.

Can you "make it?" Sure you can. Will you make it? That's up to you. You *will* have opportunities. You must seize them when they come your way. Count your many blessings, and then share them with others. Here are the key elements for you to *Graduate and Grow Rich.*

- **DREAM BIG**
- **STAY TEACHABLE**
- **STRIVE FOR PERSONAL EXCELLENCE**
- **NARROW YOUR FOCUS TO GET YOUR SUCCESS JOURNEY ON TRACK**
- **BE WILLING TO TRADE IN SOMETHING GOOD FOR SOMETHING GREAT**
- **NEVER GIVE UP ON YOURSELF**

Make the transition from security thinking to significance thinking and you will experience a life of purpose and be on track to fulfill your life's mission.

Let me close with one of my favorite stories: A little boy awakes on a Saturday morning, joyful as he finds his dad doing some work at his desk. *"Dad"*, he asks, *"Can we go out and play catch?"* Dad replies

"Sure, son, in a few minutes. Let me just finish up here."
"Sure, dad," he replied. And off he goes. Two minutes later: *"Dad, now can we go out and play catch?"* Dad, not quite finished, says, *"Just a couple more minutes, son."* *"Okay, Dad,"* and once more, he disappears.

In what seems like just a few second later, the boy re-appears, more eager than ever and, again, inquires: *"Dad, can we go now, please?"* Dad is torn. He just needs a few more minutes, yet he desperately wants to go out and play catch with his son. Over to the side of his desk, he spots a magazine. It is opened to a picture of the world.

Dad takes the picture and tears it into several pieces: *"Here, son. If you would just take this puzzle and put it together, then we can go out and play catch."* His son, still filled with enthusiasm, takes the pieces, sits at the table and devises his plan. No more than three minutes later, he returns to dad proud of his completed work.

Dad looked at the puzzle all put back together in amazement and asks his son, *"Son, how did you put the world back together so quickly?"* The little boy replied *"Oh, it was easy, dad. I just turned the picture over. On the back was a picture of some people. When I put the people back together, the world was all better, too."*

I know many of you want to change the world. And, believe me, we want that, too. By putting the best pieces of yourself together first, you will be fully equipped to make the world better.

Although young people represent only twenty percent of the population, you represent ONE HUNDRED PERCENT OF THE FUTURE. You are a force to be reckoned with. And we expect great things from you.

So, please, BE BOLD, BE PASSIONATE, and most of all, ***believe that you can.*** We believe it! And we look forward to celebrating with you as you

"Graduate and Grow Rich."

RESOURCE GUIDE

RESUMÉ WRITING

Writing a resumé for the first time is quite foreign to student. The reality is, you've never had to do it. Prepare for an exam, yes. Write a good resumé, no. So, let's go step by step, with some basics to get you started.

OBJECTIVE: First, what do you want to be? Where would you like to be in, three years or five years? Doing what kind of work?

As you answer these questions, you are defining your career objective. Avoid bland or general descriptions of your profession or skills. Give an actual description of your skills related to the job for which you are applying.

SUMMARY: A summary isolates five or six key attributes about your primary qualifications. Choose those that best demonstrate why an employer should hire you and assemble it into five or six sentences for your summary section. It is acceptable to leave off an objective if you use a clear, concise summary section.

PERSONAL INFORMATION: It is not uncommon for first time applicants to include too many details on the Personal Information section. Information like your hobbies and interest are usually irrelevant in job applications. If the interviewer wants to know more about you personally, they will ask at the interview.

WHAT ABOUT REFERENCES? Another noticeable section in newly graduates' resumé is their long list of references. No need to list references on the resume. Prepare them separately. They only need to be presented when requested by the interviewer.

BUZZ WORDS

In this world of online job searches, cyber-hires and E-Interviews, it is vital to sprinkle keywords into your resumé for optimal effect. Prospective employers, HR personnel, and recruitment agents use them in their search for the right candidate. Here are some of the most searched keywords. Use the ones most appropriate for your talents and career path.

Branding
Business Development
Change Agent
Communications
Competitive Market
Corporate Vision
Customer Retention
Decision-making
e-commerce
Strategic Planning
Entrepreneur
Entrepreneurial
Improvement

Leadership
Life-long Learning
MBA
New Media
Organizational Design
Performance
Personal Development
Product Development
Problem-solving
Project Management
Team-building

SKILLS AND EXPERIENCE

Be certain that all significant skills or experience related to the job you are applying for are included. Be sure that your resumé is free of error. Be conscious about punctuation, spelling and grammar.

Keep your sentences short and simple. We gain experience in everything we do, especially in the most important areas like maturity, emotional intelligence, creativity, communication, responsibility, determination, integrity, compassion, and problem-solving. These are the qualities employers really seek; so if you are putting together your first resumé, then look for the relevant transferable learning in your life experience and list it.

You may not have a career history, but you can certainly illustrate and prove that you have qualities gained and learned from your life experience, that employers will recognize and want. Some employers prefer fresh young people who are keen to learn, are highly committed, and who demonstrate that they possess other qualities that more experienced people may lack.

Exude a positive attitude and a cooperative spirit and you are ahead of most. Be sure to have an advisor or career counselor review the content of your resumé. Often, just one little tip can make the difference in putting your best foot forward.

Remember, a resumé is a professional document. It is the first piece of branding you. What it does is introduce you to prospective employers. Knowing this, you should prepare your resumé, so that it gives them a snapshot, yet whets their appetite to meet you and see if the position is a good fit.

Lastly, be sure to print your resumé using black ink on plain and good quality paper. Center your name at the top and never present your resume' in a plastic slide folder.

The Best Job and Career Sites listed on page 188 are an excellent source to help you build a dynamic resumé.

Sample Cover Letter
Not to be used word for word.
You must customize it for it to be seen as your own.

March 2, 20XX

Ms Mary Dodge
Intero-Bio Tech Company
Research Department
6000 Technology Drive
Cambridge, MA 02XXX

Dear Ms. Dodge:
I was referred to you by Mr. Paul Wong, a director in your Atlanta office. He informed me that your campus seeks to hire qualified individuals in your Research and Development department.

I have acquired two years of experience, including interning as researcher last year with the Atlanta campus of Questix Labs. I will be receiving my Batchelor of Science Degree this May from _____ University, graduating Magna Cum Laude.

Having interned with an entrepreneurial firm in the biotechnology field, I understand the level of commitment and cooperation required for long-term success in your industry. My background and can-do spirit will provide your department with a highly productive researcher. Should your company provide a training program for new recruits, I would welcome this completely.

I will be in the Boston area the week of April 3rd. Please call me at 404-224-2007 to arrange a convenient time when we may meet to further discuss my background in relation to your needs. If I have not heard from you by March 18th, I will contact your office to inquire as to a potential meeting date and time.

Thank you for your consideration. I look forward to meeting with you

Sincerely,

Maria Perez

SAMPLE RESUMÉ

Ashley Smith
234 Residence Hall
Your School
Your Town, NY 02000
212-333-4444
Ashley.smith@yourschool.edu

OBJECTIVE: Auditor position in public accounting in the Miami area.

SUMMARY:
- Two plus years of accounting and auditing experience.
- Auditor Internship with Ernst & Young in Boston.
- Magna Cum Laude graduate with BA in Accounting.
- Proficient with MS Office, Windows XP, and Vista.

EDUCATION:
Bachelor of Business Administration in Accounting, May 2008
Boston University, Boston, MA
Graduated Magna Cum Laude with a GPA of 3.6

Courses taken included:

Managerial Accounting	Corporate Audit & Reconciliation
Intermediate Accounting I & II	Financial Management
Accounting I & II	Internal Audit
Accounting for Not-For-Profits	Managerial Economics

EXPERIENCE:
- Auditor Internship, May /August 2007 Ernst & Young, Boston
- Participated in quarterly audit of Festiva Optics
- Received Intern of the Month award twice
- Bookkeeping Clerk, May 2008 to Present
- Hometown Bookkeeping Service, Hometown, MA
- Assisted with payroll, tax, and account processing.
- Volunteer AARP Tax Service 2005-2008

ACTIVITIES:
- Vice President, Student Accountancy Chapter, 2007-2008
- Treasurer, SIFE Students in Free Enterprise 2007-2008
- Dorm Resident Assistant, 2006-2008

References provided upon request

Best Job and Career Sites
www.jobcentral.com
www.collegerecruiter.com
www.monster.com
www.Careerbuilder.com
www.vault.com
*www.weddles.com- Publishes annual list of Best job/career sites
www.6figurejobs.com
www.theladders.com
www.Craigslist.org
www.flipdog.com
www.hoovers.com
www.wetfeet.com
www.usa.gov
www.militaryhire.com
www.execunet.com
www.vetjobs.com
www.healthcareers.com
www.diversityinc.com
www.careerjournal.com
www.computerjobs.com

Requesting a Letter of Recommendation

When requesting that a letter be written on your behalf:
1. Ask the writer if they can give you a positive recommendation. Be open to the fact that by asking you may receive a "no" as an answer. It's MUCH better to ask upfront and avoid a negative.
2. Put your request in writing, including the date by which you would like the letter completed. Last minute requests will probably not be honored - two weeks is more reasonable.
3. Provide a copy of the position, or graduate school program, to which you are applying.
4. Provide the writer with a current copy of your resumé. This will remind the writer of your unique talents, accomplishments and experiences. If there are qualities you would like emphasized, mention them to the writer so they can be considered.
5. Give the writer an addressed envelope (stamped)
6. Before you ask that your credential file be sent out, be sure all your letters have been received.
7. Thank the writer. They've given your career goal a boost!

ACE THAT INTERVIEW

Interview Tips

Understanding how to best prepare for and follow up on interviews is critical to your career success. At different times in your life, you may interview with a teacher or professor, a prospective employer, a supervisor, or a promotion or tenure committee. Just as having an excellent resumé is vital for opening the door, interviewing skills are critical for putting your best foot forward and seizing the opportunity to clearly articulate why you are the best person for the job.

Be Prepared

Successful interviews are the result of good preparation. Proper preparation will give you the information you need, and, more importantly, the confidence to succeed.

**Know Your Company ** MOST IMPORTANT

Your ability to convince an employer that you understand and are interested in their field is vitally important. Show that you have knowledge of the company and the industry. What products or services does the company offer? How is it doing? What is the competition? Demonstrate your understanding of the company: "I understand that your website was rated number one in your industry. Your company seems to be to be leader in this area, according to Business Week."

Find Out About Position Before Interview

Ask the personnel office to send you a job description. Use this information to determine what the company is looking for in applicants for the position. You will likely be asked the common question, "Why are you interested in this job?" Be prepared to answer with a reference to the company. A sample answer: "Your store has opened up several new branches in the last two years, so I believe that there is great opportunity in your organization. I also feel that I have the necessary skills and personal qualities to make a contribution."

Dress Appropriately

You never get a second chance to make a good first impression, and first impressions are lasting impressions. Non-verbal is ninety percent of communication, so dressing appropriately is of the utmost importance. Every job is different, and you should wear clothing that is appropriate for the job for which you are applying. In most situations, you will be safe if you wear clean, pressed, conservative business clothes in neutral colors.

Pay special attention to grooming. Keep make-up light and wear very little jewelry. Make certain your nails and hair are clean, trimmed, and neat. Don't carry a large purse, backpack, books, or coat. Simply carry a pad of paper, a pen, and extra copies of your résumé and letters of reference in a small folder.

Be on Time

Make certain you write down the date and time of your interview. A good first impression is important and lasting. If you arrive late, you have already said a great deal about yourself. Make certain you know where you are going and the time of the interview and allow time for parking and other preliminaries.

Be Poised and Relaxed

Avoid nervous habits like tapping your pencil, playing with your hair, or covering your mouth with your hand. Avoid littering your speech with verbal clutter such as "you know," "um," and "like."

Don't smoke, chew gum, fidget, or bite your nails. Most career development centers or public speaking classes will videotape you while being interviewed. It is excellent experience, and you can identify annoying or distracting personal habits. Use other non-verbal techniques to reinforce your confidence, such as a firm handshake and poised demeanor.

Maintain Good Eye Contact

Look your interviewer in the eye and speak with confidence. Your eyes reveal much about you; use them to show interest, confidence, and sincerity. Relax and take a deep breath. You are relating to another person, not giving a speech to a large crowd. Watch for body cues that indicate understanding and rapport.

Convey Maturity

Interviewers evaluate maturity by observing your ability to remain poised in different situations throughout the interview. Exhibit the ability to tolerate differences of opinion. Give examples of how you have assumed responsibility with little supervision. Employers greatly value maturity in their workers, because mature workers are less disruptive, require less training, and are more productive and successful than immature workers.

Avoid Being Too Familiar

Familiarity can be a barrier to a professional interview. Never call anyone by a first name unless you are asked to do so. Know the name, title, and the pronunciation of the interviewer's name and don't sit down until the interviewer does.

Be Professional

Reliability, an excellent appearance, and proper business manners are all part of professionalism. Don't ramble, or talk too much about your personal life. Example, "Tell me about yourself" is not an invitation to discuss your personal life. Also, never bad-mouth a former employer. This is unprofessional and says more about you than about them.

Answer Questions Fully

Be clear, concise, and direct. Even if the interviewer is easygoing and friendly, remember why you are there.

Relate Your Experiences to the Job

Use every question as an opportunity to show how the skills you have relate to the job. Use examples of school, previous jobs, internships, volunteer work, leadership in clubs, and experiences growing up to indicate that you have the personal qualities, aptitude, and skills needed at this new job. You want to get the point across that you are hard working, honest, dependable, loyal, a team player, and mature.

You might mention holding demanding part-time jobs while going to school, working in the family business, being president of your business club, or handling the high-pressured job of working in customer service at a department store during Christmas vacations.

Focus on What You Can Do for the Company

Don't ask about benefits, salary, or vacations until you are offered the job. This implies a "what can this company do for me" attitude. Be careful about appearing arrogant or displaying a know-it-all attitude. You are there to show how you can contribute to the organization.

Stress Your Skills

Employers look for both job-specific skills and general workplace skills. Job-specific skills are those necessary to do the particular job, like balance a budget or program a computer. General skills are transferable from school to job as well as from job to job. Foundational skills include communication, listening, problem solving, technology skills, decision making, organizing skills, planning skills, teamwork, social skills, and adaptability skills.

Be Honest

Don't overstate your accomplishments or grade point average or exaggerate your experience. Many employers verify the background of promising applicants. While it is important to be confident and stress your strengths, it is equally important to your sense of integrity to always be honest. If you haven't had a particular kind of experience, say so, but also indicate your willingness to learn new skills.

Exude a Positive Attitude

Employers want people who believe in themselves and their skills, who want to work, want to work for *them*, and have a positive attitude. An interviewee with a positive attitude conveys poise, self-confidence, and has a tendency to be more extroverted.

Employers usually choose candidates who are enthusiastic about their lives and their careers, because people perform best when they're doing what they like to do. One step toward developing a positive, enthusiastic outlook is to surround yourself with supportive, positive people.

Close the Interview on a Positive Note

The follow-up begins as you end your interview. If it is unclear to you what will happen next, *ask*. If an employer asks you to take initiative in any way, *do it*! The employer may be testing your interest in the company. Look them in the eye as you thank them for their time, shake hands, saying that you look forward to hearing from them.

Follow Up With a Letter

A follow-up letter is especially important. It serves as a reminder for the interviewer, an opportunity for you to thank the interviewer for the meeting and a chance to make a positive comment about the job opening and the company. Writing thank you notes and letters demonstrates that you have good manners and business etiquette and that you are organized (see sample at end of this section). You should seriously consider sending a personal, handwritten thank-you note in addition to the typed, more formal note. This will set you apart from the herd who will not do this.

Practice Interviewing

Like any skill, the more you practice the better you will be. Consider videotaping a practice interview. Many campuses have this service available through the career center. It is also very helpful to practice being interviewed by a friend.

Use our list of questions on the next pages for practice. Decide in advance what information and skills are pertinent to the job and reveal your strengths. For example, "I learned to get along with a variety of people when I worked for the county."

General Questions and Guides for Answering
Your Qualifications

Q. Tell me about yourself.
A. *Focus on why you would like this job and how you have prepared experientially and academically.*

Q. Why should we hire you?
A. *Focus on what your contribution will be to company success: hard work, dedication, humor. We all bring something unique.*

Q. How has your education prepared you for this position?
A. *See #1.*

Q. Do you think your grades are an accurate indication of what you have learned in college?
A. *If you don't, give examples to illustrate your answer*

Q. Tell me about one of your failures and what you learned from it.
A. *Be honest but don't bare your soul: this is not a counseling session! Demonstrate that you can use failure to achieve future success.*

Q. What do you think it takes to succeed in our company ?
A. *Reading the company's job announcement/ web page will help answer the question. If you can, talk to an employee of the company beforehand. Career fairs are excellent for this reason.*

Q. Describe your strongest communication skills.
A. *Give example. Remember, listening is key communication skill.*

Q. Think of a large task you organized. Describe the steps you followed.
A. *Use a work or school-related project to illustrate. Be specific.*

Q. Do you consider yourself a leader? Why?
A. Give an example from your participation in group projects, volunteer situations, clubs, athletics, or your work situation.

Q. Are you creative?
A. Again, give an example. Creativity is not just drawing, dancing, acting, or playing music. It is also your ability to look at things in a new way and be innovative in solving problems.

Q. Do you enjoy routine? Why? Why not?
A. Some routine is fine and necessary, like eating, going to work, etc. After that, it depends on you. Choose a job to fits your needs. If you really dislike routine, don't apply for a job that has a lot.

Q. Tell me about your computer experience.
A. Focus on what skills you have and the steps you are taking to gain more. Enthusiasm and willingness to learn are key.

Your Style and Personality

Q. How would your friends (teachers) describe you?
A. Keep it honest and positive. Remember it's not necessarily how you'd describe yourself. Your friends may see your fun and quirks. Your teacher might see your dedication and adaptability.

Q. What motivates your best work?
A. Consider the job. If you need praise or excitement or deadlines, not all jobs offer these. Give an example.

Q. How do you keep track of things you need to do?
A. You are on your own. Most answers will work, except saying that you just remember everything.

Q. Would you rather write a report or give it verbally? Why?
A. State your preference, but indicate your comfort with either approach as the situation warrants. Knowing the job requirements will assist with this question. Many jobs require both skills.

Your Interest and Commitment

Q. Why are you interested in working for our company?
A. Research into the company will pay off when answering this question. Talk about their goals for the future, their success or reputation. Back up your statement with specific examples, and include how you can contribute to the company's success.

Q. Why did you choose your major?
A. Talk about how you believed your major would increase your skills and further career goal or simply that you liked the subject matter. Mention how the skills you learned apply to the job. If you changed majors more than once, talk about what you learned about yourself from that situation and how it will help you make better decisions in the future.

Q. Do you have plans for continued study?
A. Employers are interested in people who have a commitment to life-long learning, but may not support your education plans if they are not related to the goals of the organization. Tie your own goals in with those of the employer.

Q. How do you feel about travel or relocation?
A. Know the job requirements ahead of time. Most management positions require both. Some sales and consulting jobs require extensive travel, but may allow you to return home at night.

Q. How do you deal with stress?
A. Mention your abilities to organize and prioritize ,a willingness to request supervisor's assistance, establish priorities, or stay calm in pressure situations. You might mention activities you engage in that help reduce stress, such as exercise, running, walking, working out.

Q. What area of this position would be most difficult for you?
A. Again, know the requirements. Answer truthfully, but indicate your reasons along with your willingness to perform the difficult task and how your approach to it will help minimize the difficulty.

Q. How long do you plan to stay with us?
A. As long as you can grow and contribute to their goals.

Behavioral Questions and Answers

Q. Give an example when you creatively solved a problem.
A. Creativity can be graphic design, engineering, marketing, or your ability to think outside the box. Use examples from work, homework, class, or your private life to illustrate the point.

Q. Tell me about when you went the extra mile at school.
A. Use extra credit work, study groups, volunteer activity

Q. Give me an example of a high-pressure situation you have faced this past year and how you resolved it.
A. Your ability to juggle classes, studies, part time work and career preparation are good examples

Q. Describe a situation in which you used persuasion to convince someone to see things your way.
A. Think of a school or group-related activity where you used persuasion. Describe the situation, tell what you did, and describe the result.

Q. Give me an example of a time when you set a goal and were able to meet or exceed it.
A. Work-related is best, but a goal you set personally works, too.

Q. Give me an example of a time when you tried to accomplish something and failed.
A. Remember, at the end of your story, talk about the positive things you learned from the experience and what you would do differently if given the same situation.

Q. Give an example of you showing initiative and leading.
A. Give a leadership example from school or work.

Q. Give an example of a time when you motivated someone.
A. How did you find out what motivated that person? How did you use that to accomplish positive results?

Q. Tell me about a time when you used your fact-finding skills to solve a problem.
A. Talk about which fact-finding skills you used, such as computer research, interviewing, disassembling and re-assembling, etc.

Questions You Can Ask

Choose the most appropriate questions for the situation.

Q. What are your expectations for the person you hire?

Q. Which specific skills are necessary to succeed in this job?

Q. How do my skills, experience and education differ from those of the ideal candidate?

Q. What level of input would I have in determining my objectives and deadlines?

Q. What kinds of projects might I be working on?

Q. Why do you like working for this company?

Q. What level of client contact should I expect?

Q. Would you describe the typical training program?

Q. Would I work for more than one person?

Q. Please describe the travel involved in this position.

Q. How often is relocation required for advancement?

Q. What are the advancement opportunities for this position and the typical time frame for advancements?

Q. What type of new products is the organization developing?

Q. What is your policy regarding continuing education for employees?

Q. Is there a tuition reimbursement policy?

Q. Would there be an increase in salary after completion of a higher degree? Would it make advancement easier?

Q. What are some of the biggest challenges facing your company and your plans for meeting them? or better yet,

Q. While researching your company, I read that one of your challenges is_____. How do you plan to meet this?

Q. What are your plans for expansion in the next few years?

Q. Is this a new position? If it is, why was it created? If it isn't, does the company have more than one opening?

Q. I am very interested in this position, what is the next step? *(Do not leave the interview without knowing this answer)*

Interview Day

Types of interviews

Although you should be told up front what to expect, in many cases you may be in the dark until you begin your interview. Be prepared for any of the following types of interviews.

- **Pre-screening:** Quicker and less intense than the other types, yet in many ways it's the most important type since it determines whether you'll be invited to continue in the process.
- **One person**: Done by the hiring authority such as the company president, department supervisor, school principal, etc. This can last anywhere from 30 minutes to a few hours.
- **Group:** You'll meet with several people during the course of the interview, which could last up to a day. This might mean you'll be interviewing with several people at once, or that you'll have several one-on-one interviews.
- **Several candidates at the same time:** The company may have several people interviewing at the same time. You may have some sessions together and some separate.

Some general tips:
- Every person you meet during the course of the day is a potential evaluator. Be personable and polite to everyone, and don't relax so much that your professional demeanor slips.
- Demonstrate enthusiasm, interest and confidence.
- Minimize the use of: "think", "guess", or "feel." They sound indecisive. Avoid phrases like "pretty good" or "fairly well."

Use positive words to describe your skills.
- Site specific examples how you've demonstrated your skills.
- Listen effectively, paraphrase to clarify and confirm the interviewers question, and answer what is asked.
- Talk more deliberately and articulately than usual. Most people tend to speed up their speech when they're nervous.
- Maintain reasonable eye contact; don't look down at the floor while you're contemplating an answer, or out the window.

Follow up

As soon as possible after your interview, send a letter of thanks to all the people you met and talked with that day, reaffirming your interest in the position. The letter provides one last opportunity to stand out among your competition

THE COMPANY VISIT OR SECOND INTERVIEW

Most companies recruiting on college campuses include a company visit as a part of the hiring process, after the initial screening. This visit usually consists of a day of interviewing and related activities at the company site. The visit is also called a plant trip, second interview, site visit, or office visit. There is no way to know exactly what to expect, as each company conducts their visits differently. If you're invited to visit the office or plant, be assured that you made a good impression during the initial interview, and that this trip can lead to a job offer.

The company visit serves two primary purposes:

1. Allows the company to get a more in-depth assessment of you. This is generally the last step in the selection process. Since you've already made the first cut, the employer is believes you have the skills and talents to do the job. This is a chance to show that there is a fit between you and the company culture.

2. Allows you the opportunity to see the company, meet the people, and learn more about the position.

Preparing for the Visit

Preparation for the company visit is essential. Learn as much about the company as possible.

- **Review the notes** you took after the initial campus interview
- **Annual report**
- **Check their site**; many companies have a section for grads.
- **Industry and business publications.** Sites like www.hoovers.com or www.thomasnet.com, and www.standardandpoors.com.
- **Talk with former students** now employed by the company.
- **Conduct information interviews** with people who are in the line of work for which you are interviewing
- **Talk with people** who have direct dealings with the company.

Personal Preparation

While knowledge, insightful questions and a sharp business out-look will go a long way toward impressing the employer, a lack of personal preparation can detract from your positive image.

Your appearance

Be professional (your attire, hair, skin, nails, grooming, etc.) Remember: perfume and cologne should be noticeable *only* to you, and that you need to dress appropriately to the type of company. Men: leave the earrings at home, and give some consideration to your hair length. There's plenty of time for expressing your individuality after you get a job offer!

Leave personal problems at home. Take time to clear your mind of school concerns, deadlines, family concerns, etc.

Travel

The majority of company visits are a full or half day. This usually requires an overnight stay. Generally the company will pay for everything, but not always. In the best situations, your contact person at the company will handle your travel for you, including your hotel, ground transportation and flight. If you are arranging your own travel, use a travel agent. If you prefer to handle your own travel, try www.expedia.com/ or www.travelocity.com .

In all cases, make sure you know up front how payment is going to be handled and how you will be reimbursed for expenses. A question like "Should I save my receipts?" will usually prompt your contact person to explain, but ask if unsure.

After receiving confirmation of travel arrangements, call or send a note to your contact person, confirming reservations and travel plans. Get your directions ahead of time. Ask your company contact and use MapQuest, Yahoo maps, or whichever online source you prefer. I suggest you double-check these directions with your company contact, as they sometimes are not complete.

If possible, plan to arrive in the city the night before the visit, avoiding last minute flights. This will help avoid the problems that can arise from airline delays, cancellations, weather, lost luggage, etc. Once in town, check to see if the hotel has a courtesy van from the airport. If not, keep all taxi receipts in case of later reimbursement. Large cities like Boston and New York often have subway and bus transportation. When checking into the hotel, ask for any messages (the company may have left information for you), and verify any prepayment agreements. If not prepaid, the hotel receptionist will usually require an imprint of a credit card.

Here are some other tips for your hotel stay:

- Schedule a wake-up call.
- If your room is unsatisfactory for any reason, particularly noise, don't hesitate to ask the hotel to change it.
- Non-smoking rooms are often available. If you haven't booked it in advance, ask for one upon check-in.
- Local calls are not free. They often cost anywhere from .25 to over $1.00 per call. Use your cell phone if it's personal.
- Do not bill any long distance calls to your room. Use a credit card or calling card, or your cell phone.
- Review the bill upon checkout to ensure its accuracy.
- Keep a copy, especially if you need to be reimbursed.

The Evening Before
Many companies arrange for an employee to meet the candidate for dinner upon arrival, or at a later time in the evening. The dinner is an opportunity for you to relax and meet an employee in a casual setting, while getting a feel for the next day's schedule, the company, the city, and any other pertinent topics.

Your dinner companion might be a manager, your contact person, a recent hire of the company, or alumnus. The degree of informality and the nature of the conversation can vary, but it's usually somewhat relaxed. You should still reflect maturity and professionalism, since the dinner host may be evaluating your manners, ideas and views, ability to converse, manner of speech, ability to mix business and pleasure, and maturity.

Dress appropriately for a social dinner. Eat moderately, avoid alcoholic beverages beyond one glass of wine, beer, or a single drink. Ask insightful questions and relax. Allow both your professionalism and your personality to come through.

Checking out of the hotel

As a backup to your wake-up call, set a travel alarm (your watch or cell phone works). Have a parent or friend call you in the morning to make sure you're up on time. Tardiness is the worst first impression you can possibly make. Check out before leaving for the site. If you forget, you may be charged for an extra night. Take your baggage with you.

Interview Day: what to expect

It is impossible to predict exactly what to expect because different companies set up different types of schedules. You should receive an itinerary, but be prepared for anything.

Below are some scenarios you should be ready for:
- Three to five separate interviews with various levels of management in one-on-one settings.
- The company may have scheduled multiple candidates for company visits at one time. You may engage in a combination of group sessions and one-on-one interviews during the day.
- In one-on-one interviews, expect to speak with department managers and first line supervisors.
- You may be expected to undergo some type of testing.
- Some companies have the full day determined ahead of time; others will leave it up to individuals as to what they wish to assess. Either way, all involved will meet after the process is complete to share impressions and give recommendations.
- Often a plant or business tour will be part of your day. Use the opportunity to ask insightful questions about what you observe. Note to women: just in case, bring closed-toe shoes.
- You may meet with a person to give you information about the company and evaluate some of your self-management skills

General tips for the big day

- Anyone and everyone you meet is a potential evaluator. Remain sharp, confident, and professional at all times.
- Pay attention to cues around you. You may be able to obtain valuable information in unexpected settings--- in the reception area; the company cafeteria; speaking with a receptionist.
- Interviewers scan your resumé to be familiar with your background. They look at your drive and motivation, probing for your strengths and potential weaknesses.

- Expect to be asked the same questions by three or four different people during the day. You must give as good an answer to the fourth as you do the first. This may seem tiring, but may indicate an area of particular concern to the company.
- In some instances, companies will assign each interviewer a specific quality or skill to probe during the interview. One may look for leadership ability, another for communication skills, another for a specific technical skill, and so on.
- Most companies will design the day to provide a friendly and relaxed atmosphere. Keep in mind the interview process is a two-way street; it's important to the company that you feel as comfortable as possible about the visit so that you can make an informed choice in case of an offer being tendered.
- This will be a tiring day for you--prepare for it! Guard against growing weary and neglecting your professional demeanor.
- Be ready to be offered the position, and to discuss salary.

Departure

The last meeting of the day will often be with the contact person or human resources/personnel manager. This session is to answer any final questions, explain follow-up procedures, discuss reimbursement for the company visit, talk about salary and benefits (in some cases), and take care of similar details. After the visit, be sure you know how to get back to the airport.

Most companies will structure the day to allow you to depart the facility between 3:00 and 5:00 P.M. Be sure all your questions have been answered prior to leaving, and that you know what to expect regarding follow-up to the visit.

After the Visit

As soon as possible after your visit, send a personal letter of thanks to all the people you met and talked with that day. This provides one last opportunity to stand out from your competition.

Write an additional letter to your contact person, thanking them for the effort it took to arrange your visit. Reaffirm interest in the position, highlight one or two qualifications, and show your understanding of etiquette.

The thank you letter is a business communication; in most industries this means it should be typed or emailed instead of handwritten. On average, you should hear within two weeks from the company with an offer or a rejection. However, you should find out how long you can expect to wait regarding an employment decision, and feel free to contact the company to check on delays if you don't hear within the estimated time.

NEGOTIATING YOUR SALARY AND BENEFITS

"What salary range do you expect?"
This could be one of the most difficult questions you'll be asked in an interview, if you're not prepared. Any time you walk through the door for an interview - even a first interview - you should be aware of what your education, experience and geographic prefer-ence is worth in dollar amounts. If you are unprepared for this question, you could be offered much less than you're worth. On the flip side, if you are unrealistically high in your expectations you could lose the job offer.

Initial Salary Research
Researching salary ranges can provide you with a starting point. Approach this issue in terms of a range, from the lowest salary you can accept to the highest you can expect. Check these sites:
JobSmart:www.jobsmart.org
Salary:www.salary.com
Payscale:www.payscale.com
The Riley Guide: www.rileyguide.org

When & How To Discuss Salary with An Employer
The rule of thumb is never to bring up salary yourself...*ever.* Most U.S. employers believe this makes candidates appear more concerned with salary than with the opportunity. You should wait until you've been offered a position, or until they brings it up.

With the exception of option one below, most employers will try to get you to name the first salary range, so that they can establish a starting point for negotiation. It's critical that you've done your homework, and know what you're worth.

Options you may encounter when discussing salary:

Option #1: There is no negotiation possible. This occurs when salaries are regulated by something other than the hiring manager or department, such as in government and education. In this case, salaries are often presented in a straightforward way, either in the advertisement or the first interview, as in "The salary for first year teachers is $26,500, based on the contract." In this case you just need to weigh the factors besides salary in making your decision.

Option #2: There is negotiation possible, but not invited. For example, a company may say "We would like to offer you the position of Process Engineer at a salary of $35,000."

Some possible responses might include:
• "Thank you for your offer. Before I make a final decision, could you tell me more about the benefits that are included with this salary?" "Is there someone I could contact for more information?"
• "Thank you for your offer. I think it's fair that you know that I'm considering an offer from Company B of $45,000. Is it possible for you to make up some of the difference between the offers?"
• "I am very excited about working for you, because Company A is my first choice. However, I am really looking for something in the range of $40,000 - $45,000, especially given the cost of living in Baltimore and the national median salary for this type of position. Is there any room for negotiation?"

Option #3: The company is ready and willing to negotiate.
Your first clue will be the question "what salary range are you expecting" or something like that. At this point, companies are in the budget stage, at which they'll naturally want to hire you for as little as possible.

• **BEST BET:** Include the statement "my salary is negotiable" or "I expect fair compensation for this position and geographic location" somewhere in the body of your cover letter.

SAMPLE THANK YOU LETTER

Your School
234 Residence Hall
Your Town, NY 02000
212-333-4444
ashleysmith@yourschool.com

Dr. David Jones
MetroWest Labs
5 Main Street
Cambridge, MA 02XXX

Dear Dr. Jones:

I'd like to thank you for talking with me about the research- assistant position in your Bio-Tech lab. I truly appreciate all the time and care you took in telling me about the job and learning more about me.

I am so pleased that you agree that my senior research project in seismology provides me with excellent experience for this position. I am eager to bring my passion for seismology to the research-assistant position, and I am convinced the knowledge and experience I've already cultivated make me the best researcher for the job.

I very much look forward to learning of your decision soon. Please feel free to contact me if you need more information about my qualifications.

Thank you again for the exhilarating interview.

Sincerely,

Ashley Smith

**Make sure it is written ASAP after the interview.
One week later will have little impact. **

Continuing Education

We never arrive. We are always in either a state of growth or we default to a state of demise. Continue to grow by feeding yourself with enriching, uplifting input. Experience by itself is not the best teacher...*Other* people's experience is the best teacher. Go to www.graduateandgrowrich.com for updates.

Here are some of my favorite sources for your continuing education. Your real education begins *after* graduation. Commit to life-long learning and Grow Rich!

BOOKS

Legend: **B**-Body **M**-Mind **S**-Spirit **F**-Finance

Think and Grow Rich Napoleon Hill (**M**)
How to Win Friends and Influence People Dale Carnegie (**M**)
Skill with People Les Giblin (**M**)
The Richest Man in Babylon George Clason (**F,M**)
The Magic of Thinking Big David Schwartz (**M**)
How to be Rich J Paul Getty (**F,M**)
The Seeds of Greatness Denis Waitley (**M**)
Psycho-Cybernetics Dr Maxwell Maltz (**M,S**)
Your Best Life Now Joel Osteen (**S,M**)
The 7 Habits of Highly Effective People Stephen Covey (**M**)
The Choice Og Mandino (**M**)
Greatest Salesman in The World Og Mandino (**M,F**)
Developing the Leader Within You John Maxwell (**M,F**)
The Wealthy Barber David Chilton (**F**)
E Myth Revisited Michael Gerber (**M,F**)
Who Moved my Cheese Kenneth Blanchard (**M**)
Cash Flow Quadrant Robert Kiyosaki (**F,M**)
Winning Everyday Lou Holtz (**M**)
Tuesdays with Morrie Mitch Albom (**M,S**)
You Don't Have to be Perfect John DiPietro (**M**)
Acres of Diamonds Russell Cromwell (**M**)
Rich Dad, Poor Dad Robert Kiyosaki (**F**)
Body for Life Bill Phillips (**B**)
Move Ahead with Possibility Thinking Robert Schuller (**S,M**)
What To Say When You Talk to Yourself Shad Helmstedder (**M**)

Personal and Professional Development
www.deniswaitley.com -Free Newsletter
www.FranklinCovey.com
www.joelosteen.com
www.maximumimpact.com John Maxwell -Free Newsletter
www.nightingale.com
www.positivechristianity.org -Free Daily Positive Inspiration
www.selfmarketing.com Networking -Andrea Nierenberg
www.thriveandprosper.com
www.thinkTQ.com -Free Newsletter
www.yourSuccessStore.com -Free Newsletter

Free Business Plan

www.smallbizlending.com/resources/workshop/sba

For Entrepreneurs

www.sba.gov/smallbusinessplanner
www.startupjournal.com
www.sife.org/home
www.startupnation.com
www.jumpup.intuit.com
www.e-myth.com
www.Startupsearch.org
www.Killerstartups.com
www.inc.com/resources/startup/
www.wsj.com/small-business/running-a-business
www.entrepreneur.com

Giving Back

www.ja.org
www.habitat.org
www.navigators.org
www.salvationarmyusa.org
www.goodwill.org

*All websites were checked at time of publishing.
Please send us updates or new suggested sites and we will share the best with all.

Attitude

Things turn out the best for the people who make the best of the way things turn out." **John Wooden**

Whenever I hear, 'It can't be done,' I know I'm close to success.
Michael Flatley

Ability is what you're capable of, motivation determines what you do, attitude determines how well you do it. **Lou Holtz**

I'm never down; I'm either up or getting up. **Henry Ford**

Last season, we couldn't win at home and we were losing on the road. My failure as a coach was that I couldn't think of anyplace else to play. **Harry Neale**

Most people never run far enough on their first wind to find out they've got a second. Give your dreams all you've got and you'll be amazed at the energy that comes out of you. **William James**

Overcoming/Obstacles

The human spirit is never finished when it is defeated - it is finished when it surrenders. **Ben Stein**

Identify the major obstacle that stands between you and your goal and begin today to remove it. **Brian Tracy**

Problems are opportunities in work clothes. **Henry J. Kaiser**

The most rewarding things you do in life are often the ones that look like they cannot be done. **Arnold Palmer**

When you've got something to prove, there's nothing greater than a challenge. **Terry Bradshaw**

Great spirits have always encountered violent opposition from mediocre minds.-- **Albert Einstein**

When we long for life without difficulties, remind us that oaks grow strong in contrary winds and diamonds are made under pressure. **Peter Marshall**

Quotes for the Journey

If I'd listened to critics I'd have died drunk in the gutter. **Chekov**

Although the world is full of suffering, it is also full of the overcoming of it. **Helen Keller**

Don't water your weeds. **Harvey Mackay**

Goals/Dreams

Past failure and frustration lay the foundation for understanding that created a new level of living I now enjoy. **Anthony Robbins**

In the long run, men hit only what they aim at. Therefore, they had better aim at something high. **Henry David Thoreau**

The person who makes a success of living is the one who sees his goal steadily and aims for it unswervingly **Cecil B. De Mille**

A winner concentrates on that which is goal achieving rather than tension relieving. **Denis Waitley**

Make every goal clear, specific, and time bounded **Brian Tracy**

Setting a goal is not the main thing. It's deciding how you'll go about achieving it and staying with that plan. **Tom Landry**

One mistake will never kill you. The same mistake over and over again will. **Harvey Mackay**

Better to do something imperfectly than to do nothing flawlessly. **Robert Schuller**

Don't wait for leaders. Do it alone, person to person.
Mother Theresa

You don't have to be great to get started, but you have to get started to be great." **Les Brown**

Don't wait. The time will never be just right. **Napoleon Hill**

Living/Life

There are two ways to live your life: One is as if nothing is a miracle. The other is as though everything is. **Albert Einstein**

Live as if you were to die tomorrow. Learn as if you were to live forever. **Gandhi**

People may forget what you said, or what you did, but they will never forget how you made them feel **Maya Angelou**

I kept six honest men. They taught me all I knew. Their names are What, Why, When, How, Where and Who. **Rudyard Kipling**

We are not *creatures* of circumstance; we are *creators* of circumstance. **Benjamin Disraeli**

I've learned that I still have a lot to learn. **Maya Angelou**

Act the way you'd like to be and soon you'll be the way you act. **George W. Crane**

You can't think your way into acting positively, but you can act your way into thinking positively. **Nido Qubein**

**Life is like a field of newly fallen snow;
where I choose to walk, every step will show.**

Love is a better master than duty. **Albert Einstein**

Have a little laugh at life: look around you for happiness instead of sadness. Even in darkest moments, you can find something to laugh about if you try hard enough. **Red Skelton**

Life is a boomerang. Our thoughts, deeds and words return to us sooner or later, with astounding accuracy. **Florence Shinn**

No person was ever honored for what they received. Honor has been the reward for what they gave. **Calvin Coolidge**

You can preach a better sermon with your life than with your lips. **Oliver Goldsmith**

If you judge people, you have no time to love them. **Mother Teresa**

Notes

LESSON 102
Napoleon Hill- "Think & Grow Rich"
Denis Waitley- "The Winners Edge"
Steven Covey- "The Seven Habits of Highly Effective People"

LESSON 103
David Schwartz- "Magic of Thinking Big"
Richard Bolles- "What Color is Your Parachute"
Olivia Goldsmith- "First Wives Club"
Denis Waitley- "Ten Seeds of Greatness"
Shad Helmstetter- "What to Say When You Talk to Yourself"

LESSON 201
David Schwartz- "Magic of Thinking Big"
John Gray- "Men are From Mars"

LESSON 202
Og Mandino- "The Greatest Salesman in The World"

LESSON 301
Jack & Suzy Welch- "Winning: The Answers"
Barry Posner & Jim Kouzes- "The Leadership Challenge"
Bill George- "True North"

LESSON 303
Gifford Pinchot- "Intrapreneuring"

LESSON 401
Stephen Covey- "The 8th Habit"
Harvey Mackay- "What They Don't Teach You at Harvard Business School"

LESSON 402
Dr. Andrew Weil- "Eight Weeks to Optimum Health"
Laura Lewis-"52 Ways to Live a Long and Healthy Life"

LESSON 403
Mitch Albom- "Tuesdays with Morrie"

Printed in the United States
201411BV00001B/115-333/P

9 780981 479224